Best wishes and good luck on your
journey to purpose and leadership

Kenneth E. Behring

Kenneth E. Behring

The Road to Leadership

Finding a Life of Purpose

Dedication

This book is dedicated to all of the leaders in the world and to the people who want to become leaders. Thank you for helping me find my purpose.

Acknowledgments

This book would not have been possible without the help of friends, family members and colleagues at the Global Health and Education Foundation and its philanthropic partners. Many of the stories in the book came from the reports of donors, volunteers and team members who have traveled the world to deliver the gifts of education, good health and mobility to millions of people.

I'd like to thank my editorial team for whipping my manuscript into shape: Peter Barnes, Cheryl Barnes, Joel Hodge, Diane Reeves, Nadia Skolnitsky, Amanda Larsen and Tess Civantos. Thanks to Joel, Charli Butterfield, Martha Hertelendy, and Ranky "Dabing" Chen for the photographs. Also, my thanks to the schools, museums and organizations mentioned in this book for their contributions of photos and content. I want to especially thank Cathy Gorn of National History Day for hers!

I'd also like to thank my foundation associates and business colleagues who helped make sure the facts and my recollections were accurate: Steve Beinke, Don Williams, Annette Anderson, Angie Shen, Dyan Han, Charli and Joel. Thanks to our Shanghai office for its contributions. Special thanks to my son, David, for his review and contributions.

Most of all, I'd like to thank my wife and partner for more than 60 years, Pat, for her support and for putting up with visiting editors, the days I was away from home as I worked on this book and the boxes of photographs on the kitchen table.

TABLE OF CONTENTS

My Belief
–KEB

It is not the critic who counts. Not the man who points out how the strong man stumbles or where the doer of deeds could have done better. The credit belongs to the man who is actually in the arena, whose face is marred by dust and sweat and blood, who strives valiantly, who errs and comes up short again and again, because there is no effort without error or shortcoming, but who knows the great enthusiasms, the great devotions, who spends himself for a worthy cause; who, at the best, knows, in the end, the triumph of high achievement, and who, at the worst, if he fails, at least he fails while daring greatly, so that his place shall never be with those cold and timid souls who knew neither victory nor defeat.

Theodore Roosevelt

Preface

I am a simple man who has lived a simple life and, in the process, learned a simple lesson.

I was born poor. But I will die rich—with more money, in fact, than I ever imagined existed when I was boy. By the world's standards, I climbed aboard the American dream and rode it to the top, becoming a leader in business.

Yet as I look back on all my success, I realize that doing well financially is easy compared with achieving true success: finding a purpose in life beyond just making money. Purpose is something you achieve by giving your heart, time, love and money to providing a better life for mankind.

Our world is filled with men and women who have no true purpose, no calling higher than trying to fill their bank accounts. Some chase money all of their lives, most of the time in vain. Others earn more than they will ever be able to spend, running corporations that will outlive them. Both types of people work away at what they believe is the pursuit of happiness. But they are wrong.

The world also lacks future leaders as it faces more perilous times—economically, environmentally and in international affairs. To lead, however, leaders need purpose. To lead, people need more than a lot of money, a fancy car and a big corner office.

I know how the privileged feel and how they live. My quest for riches blinded me from seeing all that I might be missing. With each moment I filled pursuing an objective I could touch—making money—I had no time to notice that I was missing something that can only be felt.

To be frank, I didn't do well in the world of feelings. But I knew people who did—people who had somehow climbed above the conflict, fear and pressure of pursuing material success and who had discovered what President Abraham Lincoln called the "better angels" of their nature and become givers and leaders. So I knew it was possible to change.

I came to call these fortunate few the "people of purpose." They are sustained by a mission for a cause greater than themselves, for a direction that gives meaning to their lives and often allows them to lead. They face each day with conviction and energy, less concerned about the pursuit of wealth and status than they are about living for a larger meaning in their lives.

I have also learned that anyone can become one of the people of purpose. Membership in this wonderful club is open to all. It is not a birthright; it is not attained by a sudden turn of good fortune or universal popularity; it has nothing to do with money and everything to do with finding and sustaining joy. Not happiness. Joy.

The simple fact is that my own discovery of purpose came long after *Forbes Magazine* listed me as one of the 400 wealthiest men in America. It came after my family was raised—my children grown with children of their own—after I had built cities and owned a professional football team, after I had lived life large in every sense of that modern and misused phrase. It came after I had suffered the irony of believing that those material successes would bring me the fulfillment I so desperately desired.

One of my first glimpses of it came in 2000, when I lifted a small Vietnamese girl from the ground and placed her in a wheelchair. In that instant, she found hope. In that instant, I saw what happens when one person imprisoned by immobility is finally able to move. I saw this little girl envision a freedom she had never known. Her face opened into a smile, her eyes as bright as the noontime sky. And I knew that as much as she had changed in that moment, I had changed even more.

For the first time I could remember, I felt joy. And I wanted to do everything in my power to keep that feeling alive. My desire for it turned me into a leader in the cause of helping end immobility in the world. This in turn made me aware that we need more leaders for more causes and convinced me to make leadership development one of my goals.

Giving a physically disabled Vietnamese girl a wheelchair did not cost me my fortune. It did not consume all of my time. What I did was something anyone can do. It was a simple process of open- ing my heart and allowing it to touch someone else through an act of kindness. Once I discovered that, my heart was open to so many more causes and opportunities to lead.

The journey to purpose and leadership is not difficult. I believe it begins with something I once heard about people: that we usually travel the path of more, better and different.

We start out wanting more. As children, teens and young adults beginning careers, we are consumed by getting as much as we can as quickly as we can. For me, a child of poverty, it was getting the basic necessities—things as simple as hot water and an indoor bathroom. (One of the reasons I pursued high school football was because school was the first place I could get a hot shower!) Once the basic necessities are covered, we work toward buying our first car, our first house and the rest.

Once we have more, we want better. As mature adults, we have the nice car, perhaps the home and furnishings, a good wardrobe and other amenities. But we are not content, so we seek houses in better neighborhoods, more expensive cars and jewelry, vacations to more exotic destinations.

As time passes and our incomes rise—perhaps the children are raised and out of the house—many of us are still unsatisfied, so we finally turn our attention to acquiring different things: not just the house in the nice neighborhood, but the biggest house in the neighborhood; not just an expensive car, but the most expensive, flashiest car; not just a nice vacation, but a weekend condo at a ski resort.

If we are fortunate enough to accumulate more money than we can spend, we shoot for *Lifestyles of the Rich and Famous*. We don't want just an expensive house, we want a 10,000-square-foot penthouse on Park Avenue in Manhattan; we don't want just an expensive car, we want the Aston Martin that James Bond drives in his movies; we don't want just a nice vacation, we want a private tour of the Hermitage in St. Petersburg. For me, different was assembling the world's largest classic car collection and buying a National Football League team, a personal yacht and my own private jet, a DC-9.

But no matter how much more, how much better, how many different things I accumulated and experienced, I had an empty feeling in my heart. No one had ever discussed purpose with me or defined it, but I knew instinctively something was missing. I was selfish and thought "things" would give me pleasure. If I had only known and experienced purpose sooner....

People of purpose have climbed above "more, better and different." They have grown to realize that beyond these three phases of life, there is a fourth—and it is by far the most important: purpose.

I deeply regret wasting so many years before finding purpose—not because I lacked the desire to find what I was looking for, but because I started out thinking it would come through financial achievement. The truth is, I had leaned my ladder against the wrong wall, realizing the mistake only when I was at the top, helplessly aware that, after a career filled with outward success, I did not even know where to look to find real happiness.

My story is one of an average man who achieved extraordinary material success doing a few simple things and then, through a random turn of events, discovered the true fountain of joy.

This is the story of my journey and my discovery. I write it around the four phases of life described above with the hope that it will help you, and that you will be able to avoid some of the mistakes I have made. And I hope that by putting you on the road to purpose and leadership, and helping you find your purpose and causes to fight for, I can help you to experience joy of your own to cherish and treasure.

Join me in that most wonderful of places—the place of purpose.

Part I

More

Chapter 1:
MY FIRST SET OF WHEELS

Be glad of life because it gives you the chance.

Henry Van Dyke

My life began in a hospital elevator in Freeport, Illinois, on June 13, 1928. My impatient arrival foreshadowed a recurring theme in my life—never waiting for things to happen, but making things happen.

It was the late 1920s and America was headed into the Great Depression. I was born in Freeport, but I grew up just across the state line in Monroe, Wisconsin. It was a small town made up mostly of Swiss and German Americans. They were from hardworking families with dairy farms that produced some of the best cheese in the world.

My parents' reach for the American Dream did not work out as well as mine did. But their struggle laid the foundation for my later success. They had lost their farm some years before I was born.

To provide for our family, my father, Elmer, moved to Monroe to take a job in his brother-in-law's lumberyard. He worked for 25 cents an hour. To make extra money, my mother, Mae, cleaned houses for other families, took in laundry and hung wallpaper with her cousin.

We were poor, but we always had food on the table. Pretty much the same thing every night—fried potatoes and cucumbers. They came from our big garden in the backyard. Sometimes we had meat. We rented a house for $12 a month. The neighborhood was built between the brewery, the cheese factory, a coal yard and the noisy railroad tracks. The house had no hot water or central heat. When my father's dad died, he inherited $1,200. He used that money to buy the house.

My father worked long hours, walking to and from the lumberyard twice a day. It was painful for him—he had a clubfoot that never healed after a botched operation. Even when the temperature dropped to 20 degrees below zero, he would walk in the snow and ice. He came home for lunch because it was the only place he could afford a hot meal.

In the winter, I slept in the cold. A pot-bellied stove in the kitchen was two rooms away, behind two sets of doors. I had only blankets to keep me warm when the temperature outside dropped below zero. If I wanted a hot bath, I had to heat up the water myself on the stove. For much of my childhood, the only clothes I wore were a pair of overalls. Our car was old and did not run most of the time.

Our home was filled with the stress of making ends meet. There was little time for the idle conversation, family activities and affection that bring parents and children together. I think that was the case because my parents were older when I was born. My father was 39, my mother was 32. My sister was older, too—13 years my senior. I was the family tagalong, arriving at a time when my parents were just trying to survive.

They didn't have big dreams. I guess their dreams died when

they lost their farm. So I wasn't supposed to dream, either. But I did.

I dreamed of getting out of Monroe someday. I knew there was another world outside my town. I knew that from the newsreels at the movie theater and from Buck Rogers. But my parents said dreams would lead only to disappointment. They told me, "You're poor, Kenneth. You can't do those things you talk about, so forget it." I remember my mother telling me, "You'd better develop a personality. You are not going to make it on your looks." I must have looked hurt, because she turned away quickly, back to her stove.

I can remember every detail about that moment more than 70 years ago. I suppose she was giving me the best advice she could at the time, given our situation and our potential in Monroe. But I also know that my parents weren't equipped to teach me about achieving dreams.

Despite our struggle, I never felt deprived. Almost everybody was in the same boat in the Depression. In fact, I feel I had a happy childhood. I remember the pleasures of small-town life: picnics with relatives; riding with my cousins on the flatbed of my uncle's truck to a lake; spending the day fishing; schoolboy crushes; and going hunting along the railroad track for rabbit, pheasant and squirrel, which provided food for the family. I enjoyed tracking animals and figuring out how to outsmart them; I also enjoyed fishing in streams, creeks and lakes nearby.

The only thing that my parents ever forced me to do was study music and take lessons. They chose the accordion, of all things. I thought it was foolish. I kept thinking, "The music lesson money is taking away from our food money." Fortunately, any musical ambitions I might have had ended when I entered the Monroe Music Competition. I was the only accordion player to enter the contest, and the judge awarded me second place. I had to have been pretty bad to win second place in a competition with only one contestant.

The greatest trauma of my childhood was a serious accident. I was 10 years old when a car struck me as I crossed the street. The collision fractured my skull. I was in a coma for a week. I drifted between life and death. When I recovered, I could not remember the accident. The injuries were so serious that I had to learn to walk all over again.

A lot of the conditions of my childhood were beyond my control. But I was not going to let that stop me. I felt special. I felt different from my parents and my neighbors. I wasn't going to let my parents' attitudes prevent me from reaching my goals. We weren't on the same page at any time. They were nice people, but I wasn't proud of them. We rarely talked about anything. I learned to eat fast so I could leave the table and get going.

So I became independent at a very young age. I started making decisions for myself when I was six years old, when I began to work odd jobs. I caught nightcrawlers and sold them for a nickel a can.

As soon as I was old enough to push a lawnmower, I mowed lawns at night and on weekends to earn money. I would approach a neighbor, even strangers, and ask if I could mow the lawn for a quarter—or 50 cents if it was big. I got a job as a caddy at the local golf course. It paid 35 cents a round.

But I really got going as a small businessperson when my parents gave me a bicycle. They cashed in a life insurance policy they had taken out on me when I was born. I didn't care about the life insurance policy—I wanted a bicycle. Really bad. And the policy was the only source of money my parents could tap to enable them to buy me a bike.

It was a big deal. The bike cost $28, a small fortune in the Depression. And it was one of the nicest models—not a cheap one. That was the start of a lifelong pattern—I wanted the best. I didn't want anyone to have a better bicycle. It was a two-tone brown Schwinn with a big basket. It also had a light on the handlebars so

I could ride it before dawn. That was important, because it allowed me to make money off my bike. It was the greatest thing that had happened to me to that point.

At 10 years old, I started working for a local cheese maker before school. I would get out of bed around 4 a.m. and bike to the factory.

I worked with about 20 farms. Farmers would milk their cows and bring the milk to the factory in large cans. Then I would help the farmers unload the containers. The factory paid me 10 cents an hour.

With that bicycle, I landed my first true job, with the *Milwaukee Journal*. I got a paper route. I started to sell—one penny for every paper I sold or delivered, two pennies for the Sunday edition.

I began to shape my future. For the first time, I saw how real money was made. And through trial and error, I learned about strategy. Within a short time, I learned to take my load of papers into town and set up sales right outside the drugstore—or as close as I could get without having the owner chase me away. That's where the customers were. At 11 years old, I'd learned my first lesson in business: location, location, location.

That bicycle gave me freedom and mobility for the first time. I could go further, much faster, and I began to appreciate the use of time. Early on, I learned how to be productive. (Little did I know that wheels would also play an important part in my life decades later.) I started giving money to my parents to help them with expenses at home.

I got other jobs. At age 12, I went to work at a local grocery store. At first, I had to stock the shelves. But I begged to do sales. Farmers would bring their eggs to the store and we'd have to count them. Then the farmers would exchange their eggs for groceries. I loved encouraging them to trade their eggs for all the groceries they could take so the store would get as many eggs as possible to resell to other customers. I eventually earned 25 cents an hour in this job, and that was significant: it was the same wage my father was making at the time. Starting at age 14, I made more money loading 50-pound bags of concrete mix from boxcars to trucks in my uncle's lumber-yard in the summer. I started out making 25 cents an hour, but even-tually I made 50 cents an hour, twice as much as my father. But he never complained to my uncle about his pay; I guess he did not want to risk losing his job.

At age 16, I landed a job at the local Montgomery Ward store. From my work at the grocery store, I knew I loved people and sell-ing. I was good at it, and I could make more money at Montgomery Ward selling on commission. It certainly beat lifting cheese at the cheese factory or loading concrete mix into boxcars. I guess I did a pretty good job in a short time. I wasn't there more than two weeks when the manager put me in charge of two departments, sporting goods and paint.

I always tried to turn a $5 sale into a $100 sale. A customer would come into the store to buy paint for one room and I would say to him, "I think you could make your house worth more if you'd paint the outside. And our paint is a reasonable cost. You can finance it and we'll deliver it to you. You could make your house worth a lot of money." I got a lot of people to paint their barns, too. Or someone would want to buy a cheap fishing reel and I would tell him, "You can't catch a fish with this reel. You need a good reel."

Selling was partly a natural gift. But I also learned quickly never to spend time on people we called "tire-kickers." You could identify them by listening and asking questions. If you got one, you immedi-ately turned him over to someone else. When I got a bona fide cus-tomer, I'd learn how much they were willing to spend, also by listening and asking questions. A good salesman talks to a customer only after he listens. I learned to zero in on the customer's needs and then provide the product. I have watched too many salespeople "oversell," meaning that once they got someone ready to purchase, they kept on selling and eventually talked the customer out of buying. Once you write up the order, don't try adding more. You can talk customers right out of their purchases.

Sometimes the store wouldn't stock an item a customer wanted. I knew that was an opportunity for me. I set up my own sporting-goods business on the side. I ran it out of my house. Guns, motors, fishing boats—I knew there was a demand, and I found the supply. On weekends, I'd drive to nearby cities and towns and buy the items at retail. Then I'd come home and resell them to my local customers at a markup. I saw it not only as a good business, but also as doing people a favor. I was making more from home than I was at Montgomery Ward.

While I was at it with sporting goods, I started selling cars. I bought my first car, a 1928 Pontiac, for $80 when I was 15. Someone ran into it. I got $100 from the insurance claim and bought used parts to fix it. (I traded my bike for the labor.) I still had the car and traded it for another. I was in business. I'd purchase two wrecked vehicles that were damaged in different areas and have a small body shop rebuild them into one car. Dealing in cars was the first time I could see making money without physical labor.

As soon as I got any money at all, I started another lifelong pattern: buying things. I bought my first car. I bought my parents their first radio. I would look at the catalog in our outhouse, at the guns and fishing poles. I couldn't wait to have a big car, the best fishing pole, the best whatever. I wanted better than I had. As a child growing up in the Depression, my dreams were focused on things that I could acquire or achieve.

I was hungry. When you have less, you are hungrier—for achievement, for things, for success. And that hunger stayed with me all of my life, motivating me to work harder and achieve more. With my bike, my car, my jobs and my ambition, I learned that nothing is impossible.

Even then, I knew I was looking for something. I just didn't know what it was.

Today, I think that I was fortunate to have the parents I had.

They gave me what I needed most—independence. Trying to survive in the Depression prevented them from spending time with me. But that gave me the freedom to explore and grow on my own. I learned how to make decisions for myself. I learned a lot quickly. I came to appreciate that there is no meaningless activity, just as there is no meaningless acquaintance. There are no empty actions. I learned that each one led somewhere. And I enjoyed that. I can recall that even before my teenage years, I became aware that activity and relationships led somewhere. I appreciated that idea long before I understood what it was, or what it could do for a person with ambition. That early experience helped me later in business, where leadership and decision-making skills are so critical.

My friends experienced that, too. The difference was that as we grew up, many of them seemed to become satisfied with what they were doing and turned it into a career. Once in a while, I wished I could be satisfied like them. They seemed content. They were good people, hardworking and enjoyable to be with. Many remain close to me today. They were able to settle into comfortable existences. They led lives that were every bit as fulfilling for them as the life I imagined and wanted.

Why couldn't I be content? Even now, 70 years after I first had those feelings, I wonder what it was that has never let me stop and rest, even for a short time. My father never spoke of unfulfilled dreams. My mother did her best to limit my hopes. My closest relatives were happy in their blue-collar jobs. I didn't learn about dissatisfaction from any of them.

So where did my powerful drive come from? Perhaps from that terrible accident that almost took my life. Perhaps our poverty. Perhaps the lack of love and affection from my parents. I don't know.

Whatever the reason, I didn't understand the root of it. In fact, I wouldn't know for another 60 years. All I realized was that I was missing something. At a young age, I began searching for activities and things to fill the void in my heart. I needed to find a sense of fulfillment.

I think it's obvious that my first experience in filling that void came through work. Not only did I feel useful, I felt necessary. I was helping my parents. Work gave me a sense of accomplishment and moving ahead. It gave me a feeling of self-importance. It was as if the harder I worked, the more important I became, to myself and to those who depended on me. I also began to learn that the harder I worked, the more fortunate I was.

My work in those early years was menial. Years later, my sons could not understand how I could have been gratified with mowing lawns or carrying golf clubs. I can't blame them. Those jobs were boring and often thankless. But at that point in my life, I performed them with pride and dedication. I knew how I felt when I was working. Time seemed to matter. Actions had consequences. Conditions were changed. At a basic level, lives were improved. There was power in work.

It didn't matter to me what a man did, only that he was a hard worker and was honorable. My father was both. Years later, I came to realize that the difference between us had nothing to do with how hard we worked, or how intelligent we were, or even our abilities.

The difference was that I was never satisfied—at least not for long.

In time, after every new experience or job, I would become bored. I'd need to explore better opportunities.

I had the freedom to do this because my family did not depend on me as the sole breadwinner. I was able to take risks that my father could not. Already he had lost our farm, and I am sure that event shook his confidence, though we never spoke about it. As he aged, security became more important to him than reward. My father never learned one of my own most important lessons—real reward comes only with risk.

I found freedom in work. But I did not enjoy every minute of every job. There were hours of drudgery, sometimes followed by hours of physical pain. The summer I worked loading the 50-pound bags of concrete mix for my uncle, the temperature inside those boxcars would often climb to more than 100 degrees. We would work long days, resting only once in a while. At night, I'd walk home. My body ached in places that had never ached before. Each morning I'd wake up stiff and sore, counting the days until Sunday, when I could have one day to myself. It was a miserable summer, but the experience proved important to my future. Yet again, the hard work would pay off.

I was a teenager. I was 5 feet 10 inches and 195 pounds, with short legs and a low center of gravity. The physical labor hardened me, increasing my coordination and power. The bad working conditions disciplined me to heat and exhaustion. I learned not to complain. I just did my job.

I don't know how I made it through that summer. But when fall arrived, I had the opportunity to join the football team. And I was ready. For all of the boredom and pain, that summer job was one of the most important experiences of my young life. I didn't realize it at the time, but my hard labor was preparing me for a success that, more than anything up to that point in my life, would define who I was and what I would become.

Chapter 2:
THE PLAYING FIELD

Build up your weaknesses
until they become your strong points.

Knute Rockne

I learned a lot about life from football. As a teenager, I loved the game. I couldn't wait from one season to the next. Football gave me satisfaction. It let me use my inborn ability. It built my competitiveness. And for the first time, my peers and older people alike recognized me. I liked that then, and I still do.

But football gave me much more.

Football was big in Monroe, one of the few diversions people in a small town could enjoy. At 195 pounds, I was the biggest player on my team, the Monroe High "Cheesemakers." I was strong and a good sprinter. "Built for football," my yearbook said. On offense, I was a running back, and on defense, I was a linebacker. And I loved to hit. I learned that intimidation was a great advantage on the field. I found out that if you hit your opponents harder than they hit you, you never got hurt.

I wasn't the best athlete, but I gave 120 percent every time I played. I always played 60 minutes of each contest. I never came out. One time, I was stuck in bed with a bad flu. But our game that week was against the best team in the conference. I climbed out of bed and went to the field. My teammates were afraid I wasn't going to make it, but my showing up gave them more confidence. I didn't play my best that day, but it was enough to help our team win.

I developed my competitiveness in sports early on—hunting, fishing, swimming. When I was 10, I played sports with a girl from a wealthy family in town. She was a year older than I was, a tomboy and a terrific athlete. She was tougher than anyone I ever played. I had to work hard to keep up with her. If she beat me at tennis, I'd keep coming back. I'd watch her playing tennis with her friends, trying to zero in on her weaknesses. She taught me to try harder and to uncover opponents' weak spots. Eventually, I found hers and learned to beat her.

I had a high tolerance for pain. The hot boxcars of my summer job had taught me not to think about it. I could control it. I thought positively. I took all of that to the football field and discovered that long practices and hard work didn't wear me down like it did my teammates. I enjoyed practices. I often felt more energy afterward than before they began. I hated games to end. I guess this showed in my attitude, because I was captain of the team before long. I was often in the headlines of the local sports page. "Behring Named Among Wisconsin Grid Leaders," one headline read.

For some reason, in my freshman season, I purchased the largest pair of shoes I could find. They were five sizes too big. I stuffed the toes with cotton to try to make them fit. I don't know what I was thinking. Halfway through the season, my coach took me out of play in the middle of a game. He ordered me to remove my ridiculous "clown shoes" and put on a smaller pair that fit. He took the smaller shoes from one of my teammates and just gave them to me. My performance improved immediately.

Maybe I wanted those larger shoes because they made me feel bigger and more important. I will leave that to the psychologists to decide. But I'm sure those oversized shoes tell more about my personality back then than I really want to know.

Our playbook was not sophisticated. I would say it was four yards and a cloud of dust, except that football seasons in Wisconsin were mostly mud. I soon learned that my short legs gave me the competitive advantage. I had better leverage to go head to head in the mud. I was given the ball two out of four downs and sent crashing through the line—right and left—over the guards and tackles, or around the end. I used to fight for every inch. One game, the rain and mud were so thick that the other team wanted to cancel. My coaches insisted we continue; they understood our advantage in the mud. I ran for a record that night, even though the other team targeted me. The defense tackled me on every down, whether I had the ball or not.

In those days, natural ability was about all anybody had. We didn't have the sophisticated training tools athletes use today. There were no weight rooms, no trainers, no dietary supplements or cross-training strategies. But there were hot showers. Football provided me, for the first time in my life, with a hot shower. I knew about hot water and indoor plumbing, naturally. But we didn't have that in our home. We had the old water pump in the front yard. It provided two things: cold water for the family and a place to tie up Butch, my pointer. He never learned to point to the day he died.

One player, Eugene Davis, taught me that natural ability isn't required for success. At 135 pounds, Eugene didn't fit the mold of a classic football player. Physically, you'd think he was better suited for the chess team—a fair-haired kid with intense concentration. But Eugene's build and look were only part of the story.

His heart was bigger than Lake Michigan. As a blocking back, he would throw himself against bigger opponents on the line. He didn't seem to care about hurting himself. He'd open up holes for me to run through, then return to the huddle to get his instructions and do it all over again. I can't remember Eugene carrying the ball my entire senior year, and I can't remember him once complaining. With his small size in the offensive backfield, and playing corner-back on defense, he reminded me many times of a killer bee: out of nowhere, he would come up and sting players more than twice his size. Sometimes he'd lay them out flat.

Often the most tenacious and successful people will be those you least expect, those who play from the heart. Eugene was the first person I met who helped me understand this. Since then, I've come to recognize the quality of an exceptional heart almost instantly. There is something in the individual's face, a clear-eyed honest enthusiasm that becomes infectious to the rest of the team.

Football games were rarely physically painful for me. I had those hot boxcars to thank for that. But they were emotionally painful, at first. It seemed that just about everybody came out to support the team—except my parents.

It upset me that my parents didn't attend my games. The school gave players free tickets for parents. I would leave them on the kitchen table at home and mention them to my mother and father. Early on, I would search the stands, hoping they would be there. But they never came. I was disappointed and hurt.

But in hindsight, I can't blame them. My dad was tired when he came home. He couldn't leave work early for games because he couldn't afford to lose his 25-cents-an-hour job. For one thing, we were always in debt to the grocery store. A few years later, I found out that my parents never got ahead of their food debts and that they still owed money to the grocer. (I paid off that bill myself.)

So after a while, I stopped looking for them in the stands.

I reminded myself that they really couldn't afford free time. But from that experience, I started to think about money and the freedom it could buy. Long before I was successful, I knew from the experience of missing my parents at games that time and money were connected: Not only is time money, but money provides time.

Football also taught me about leadership. I was bigger than my teammates, so that helped me take charge. And I wanted to take charge. I wasn't the quarterback, but I basically called the shots. Our quarterback, a friend of mine, was a good athlete and a good guy. But I was afraid he wasn't going to call on me often enough, and I wanted the ball every down. In the huddle, if he made a call I didn't like, I would override him. The other players would just go along with it. I wanted to be in every play. I loved running.

I must have learned something on the field. On Valentine's Day 1946, our schoolmates gathered in the gym to honor our team for winning the conference championship my senior year. Our coach, Howard Sharp, and principal, T.R. Holyoke, handed out miniature golden football trophies and varsity letters. It was nice to be recognized.

I also exercised leadership off the field. I am not especially proud of one experience. But I learned something from that, too.

My class had three months until graduation. We felt things slowing down, including our physical education classes. Because we were so close to the coaches through sports, gym class was pretty informal. It was the end of the year. We were bored. Our coaches looked the other way. So my friends and I often skipped gym to cross the street to a local bar.

One spring day, however, we got a little too comfortable at the bar. We all had maybe one too many beers. Time got away from us. Before we knew it, gym was over and we were late to our next period. By the time we showed up at class, we were doing our best to keep the smell of alcohol off our breath. But our teacher wouldn't let us into the room. Whether someone had told her where we had been or whether she simply knew from our behavior, I can't remember. But I do recall that she demanded we leave. She suspended us for our behavior.

I should have accepted my punishment and returned to school the following day, sorry for my behavior. I deserved to be suspended. But I was arrogant and full of myself. I took the leadership skills I had developed in the three previous years and came up with a plan to get back at the school. With a friend, Harold Davidson, I organized a strike—a student walkout. But not to protest my suspension—I knew my classmates wouldn't go for that.

I found a better cause. Earlier, the school had announced that Coach Sharp was going to be let go to make room for Coach Don Huddleston, who was returning from World War II. It was a commitment the school had made to Coach Huddleston, though Coach Sharp had taken us to the conference championship. And it was a commitment the school was going to keep.

I knew there was enough support among my classmates to organize a strike on behalf of Coach Sharp. And that's what I did. Word spread instantly. The next day, the town square filled with hundreds of students marching, chanting and holding signs. They demanded that the school keep Coach Sharp.

It was dishonest; it was wrong. But it succeeded in keeping the students out of class for days, at least until our school superintendent, E. O. Evans, called me to his office. He asked me to call off the strike and get students back to school.

While I had initiated the strike under false pretenses, I did learn a valuable lesson from Superintendent Evans. The walkout had embarrassed him and challenged his leadership. But he didn't get angry or confront me. Instead, he approached me on two more effective levels: he appealed to our personal relationship and he appealed to my reason.

His son was a friend of mine. I'd spent many hours at the Evans home, and the superintendent had always been kind to me.

He began our conversation by reminding me of that relationship. He put my actions and their consequences within that framework. He got me to agree that we did have a good relationship and that we could be considered friends. Then he got to the heart of the issue: a commitment had been made to Coach Huddleston.

The coach had served our country in the war and brought honor to Monroe. Superintendent Evans had made him a promise. I couldn't argue. I was about to back off when he made his final point. I was surprised. It forced me to surrender completely.

Evans said he knew what had happened the day I called the strike. He'd spoken with the teacher. He knew my motives were wrong. But then he made me an offer I couldn't refuse. He said he'd let me back into class without further punishment for my trip to the bar. I agreed. The strike was over. Students returned to school. But my regret through the years about the incident was magnified by that fact that in the end, Don Huddleston never came back to Monroe. I don't know why. But I have often wondered whether it was because of the strike and my bad behavior. If it was, I want to sincerely say now, "I'm sorry, Coach."

Since then, I've observed that a charismatic personality and a willingness to take risks only for personal gain do not make a good leader. Principle-centered leadership is based on selfless courage, practical wisdom and moral objectives. It's based on honesty and is focused on achieving what is best for others, whether they understand it or not. Consequently, great leaders are not always popular, but they are consistent. Opinion polls, conventional wisdom and difficult endeavors don't affect them. Their vision exceeds the horizon, and they have the ability to put momentary action and current affairs in a larger, more meaningful context.

Though these lessons have been often repeated, they made their first and most indelible impression on the Monroe High School football field. I was about to begin applying them in the "real" world.

My baby picture, 1928

My parents, Elmer and Mae Behring, in the 1920s. The stern expressions were typical of their Swiss-German heritage.

Boy Scout Behring, Troop 114, Monroe, Wisconsin, about 1939. Still a little thin for football.

Me at age 18, captain of the high school football team. Below, a ticket to a game, like the ones I used to leave on the kitchen table for my parents.

Monroe

High School

FOOTBALL

ADULT TICKET

Adm. 33c, tax 7c
Total 40c

The Cheesemakers of Monroe High School, 1945. I've got the ball.

High school graduation pictures for me and Pat, 1946.

Cutting the cake at our wedding in 1949

*One of my first cars, a 1939 Buick Century. My passion for
cars was well developed by the time of this picture.*

*After I started my own used cars lot, I went into business
with my father-in-law, Budd Riffle.*

The house I grew up in.

My first car dealership, Lincoln-Mercury.

I am in business as a homebuilder in Florida, 1957. My first three sons, Tom, David, and Michael.

Our first house in Florida—I built it.

Pat and I relaxing at our house in "The Woodlands" in Tamarac.

Jackie Gleason and me at a press conference at our Woodlands home, 1969.

Our Modiflex factory in Tamarac.

I made sure I spent a lot of time with residents of Tamarac.

Umpiring at a baseball game at Tamarac. The glasses helped me call the pitches.

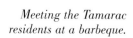

Party invitation— Life begins at 40, 1968.

Meeting the Tamarac residents at a barbeque.

The boys in Florida, 1962: Jeff, Tom holding Scott, Michael and David.

The boys grown up— Jeff, David, Scott, Tom and Michael.

David Behring, #32, playing football for Pine Crest School.

In the Seahawks locker room at the Kingdome in Seattle.

On the sidelines for a Seahawks game.

Carrying the ball at the headquarters of the Seattle Seahawks.

The Blackhawk ranch, soon to become a community.

Blackhawk, under construction 1976

Hitting the links with my good friend, Ken Hofmann.

A marlin, more than 1,000 lbs., I caught in Australia

A 21-foot, 3500 lb. crocodile I took in Tanzania.

A 12-point elk I took in Colorado.

My first classic car, a 1937 Cord Sportsman.

Jay Leno, a classic car lover, joins Pat and I at the opening of our car museum.

This was the event for the launch of my latest real estate venture with a Chinese partner, a high-end development in Shanghai called "The Sanctuary at Dongtan."

Pat and I with our grandchildren in 2012.

My friend, Mexican billionaire Carlos Slim, has partnered with me to distribute free wheelchairs in Mexico.

With my good friend, King Juan Carlos of Spain.

Pat and I with former President Bush.

With former President Clinton on my plane.

Chapter 3:
THE CHICKEN COOP

The man who will use his skill
and constructive imagination to see how much
he can give for a dollar, instead of how little he can
give for a dollar, is bound to succeed.

Henry Ford

My plan out of high school was to play football at the University
of Wisconsin. I had been encouraged by a coach to compete at the
college level. My friend Harold Davidson and I invested $35 in a
tiny trailer that we pulled behind a car to Madison. We parked in the
back of a service station near campus, paying the owner $3 a month
to supply us with water, electricity and a bathroom.

Madison was beautiful in the fall. The campus was busy. I
enjoyed being part of a big college football program. But my college
career ended quickly. In preseason training, I blew out my knee.
Without the chance of an athletic scholarship, I knew staying at
school would be almost impossible. The war had ended and upper
classmen were returning from service; financial aid was hard to
come by. I just didn't have the resources to stay. I dropped out after
one semester. My decision to move on became easier in the winter,

when our trailer became an icebox. The heater could take only
enough fuel to stay on for three hours at most. It was almost impossible to sleep at night.

Quitting college was a big turning point in my life. It was one of
the few times I felt indecision. I almost gave it one more try: one of
my freshman coaches was a former colonel in the Marine Corps and
had graduated from the Naval Academy in Annapolis. He suggested
I transfer there, rather than give up on college altogether. I had
passed the university athletic program's toughest physical exam, so I
felt I could handle Annapolis. And it seemed like a good idea to go.
So I hit the road. I drove 300 miles before I had a change of heart. I
turned around and drove back home to Monroe. On a stretch of road
somewhere, I realized I couldn't live under the tight restrictions of
college, let alone a military school. I knew then I wanted to get to
work and make money. I knew I wanted to go into business for
myself and would never work for a corporation, so I really didn't
need a college degree anyway. And I was impatient—I didn't want to
wait three and a half years to start my career.

Before I left school, I managed to complete a few courses. One
was "City Planning." The professor asked me if I had transferred
from another college, as he hadn't seen me on campus before.
I replied that I was a freshman. He was shocked—he told me the
class was only for seniors. But he let me stay. For one assignment,
I planned a complete city. Later on in life, I would build a city from
scratch in Florida. I guess I got something out of college after all.

I have no regrets about my limited college experience except for
one thing: I miss the network of friends and classmates that stays in
touch after graduation. And I did finally get a degree—an honorary
doctorate from Brigham Young University in 2002, in recognition of
my philanthropy and business success.

After high school, one of my best friends, Dick Bienema, took off
to join the Coast Guard. Like me, he needed to make his own way in

life. He, too, had grown up on the wrong side of the tracks. After his mother died, his father married a woman who refused to raise Dick because he served as a reminder of the previous wife. Dick's father had a good job and could have taken care of him. But the new wife would not allow it, and he was shipped to his grandparents in Monroe. They lived on public assistance.

Dick became an immediate friend through school. We met when we got into an argument over who would play a position on the softball team. His great personality and his sense of adventure impressed me. He had been cut off from his father. He watched stepbrothers and stepsisters receive the love and opportunities that he would never know. But he refused to let that defeat him. He simply kept moving forward in his life. After the Coast Guard, he got a good job as a mason.

Dick and other friends beginning their careers inspired me. I assessed my professional options. After football, my passion was cars. My years working at Montgomery Ward and my experience trading cars had taught me how to sell, how to read customers, how to focus on their needs and help them make the necessary connections to complete a sale. So I decided to become an automobile salesman.

A friend of mine who had worked with me at Montgomery Ward had left for a job at the local Hudson dealership. She got a hold of me when she heard I was back in town, telling me that the dealer was desperate for a good salesman. But Hudsons were not easy to sell (they were one of the biggest product bombs in the history of American business). So six months later, I went to work for the local Chevrolet dealer. For my dollar, Chevrolet was manufacturing the best cars in 1948 and 1949, including the line of trucks that were in demand in Monroe. The owner paid me a 25 percent commission on gross profit and included me on business decisions. He allowed me to travel, buy new cars from other dealers and bring them back to

Monroe. My lifelong interest in cars gave me a good eye for what customers wanted. Soon, I was making more in commissions than his son and son-in-law, who managed the dealership. They decided to cut my commissions from gross profits to net profits (after overhead), which cut my paycheck by half. I decided to quit. They were left without their top salesman, and their business suffered. There was a saying in Monroe: "You feed the pigs, but you send the hogs to market." They had gotten greedy, and now they were suffering the consequences.

After two years with the Chevy dealership, I moved to a Chrysler dealership. Ernest Studer, a hardworking and honest man with a large family, owned it. He also gave me the latitude to buy inventory. I also managed the used car business. But I soon realized that his first love was farm machinery, and his objective was to get out of car sales. So I saw there was also no future there.

I knew one thing for sure: I was disappointed in working for oth- ers. So I had an idea for my own company, Behring Motors. Now, at age 21 and four years out of high school, I felt I could not rely on somebody else for my living. I wanted to do what I wanted to do, as fast as I could. My employers had not been fast movers. I had learned this in a short time: Most people think about things and then do them. I do things and then think about them. Ready, fire, aim. I realized I would not be as successful as I wanted to be working for someone else.

My father had worked for others. I admired him in a way. He was a good employee and a stable provider. When I worked for the Chevy and Chrysler dealerships, I tried to be the kind of employee my father had been—always there, always on time. And I quickly came to appreciate the feeling of security. I could have stayed with them forever and made a good living. The Chevy dealership was pay- ing me almost $10,000 a year, a nice income in Monroe in the 1940s.

It was also plenty to support a wife and family. I had known Pat Riffle briefly in high school. She had dated my good friend Jerry Schwaiger and had set me up on a double date with one of her girl-friends. But her friend and I didn't click, and I resented her a bit for putting me with someone I wasn't interested in.

After high school, Pat worked upstairs in the accounting office at Montgomery Ward. I worked the floor in sales and counted every commission in my head even before a sale was completed. On pay-day, I could estimate to within a dime how much my paycheck would be. I got angry at Pat one payday when the check came up short. Standing above her desk, I all but accused her of cheating me out of my commission. I was impressed when she smiled and calmly answered that she would look into it immediately and, if there was a problem, take care of it directly. There was a problem. She fixed it.

I was too impulsive to be embarrassed, but not too embarrassed to ask her out after my return from college. She had been dating a friend of mine, the son of Monroe's chief of police. But that didn't stop me. Our first date was a dance at Lake Delvin. The woods were cool, and the dance floor was lit up by lightbulbs strung post to post. A big band played popular songs by Tommy Dorsey, Artie Shaw and Glenn Miller. As she had that day in her office, Pat impressed me with her confidence. She seemed at ease with me. She did not appear too impressed, either. I mean, I was the top-selling car sales-man in Monroe—perhaps even the county! And I now drove one of the nicer cars—a bright yellow 1948 Buick convertible I had bought a year earlier. She was quiet, but she seemed genuinely interested in me and my observations about life.

We enjoyed the evening together. But she surprised me when I pulled up in front of her house. She immediately jumped out and ran inside—not even a "good night." I wasn't used to that. I pulled away from the curb wondering what I had done. Did I miss something? Hadn't we had a good time? As I drove away, I went over the evening in my mind, the conversations and activity. Had I said something wrong? Not paid enough attention to her? Did one of my friends say something?

She solved the mystery the following morning. She called to apologize for her abrupt departure—she said she'd simply gone too long without a powder room break. I said I understood and asked her out a second time. She accepted, and we continued our romance through the summer. Her stepmother warned her about my type. "I wouldn't fall in love with him," she said. "All he'll do in life is hunt and fish and go bald." She was right on every account. Despite her concerns, Pat and I fell in love. We were married on October 16, 1949. She was 20 and I was 21.

From the beginning, it was clear that Pat was the only girl for me. She was supportive in every way and willing to do whatever I needed, providing me with freedom and flexibility. I would need it as I made plans to build my own used car dealership, from the hubcaps up.

I talked the owner of the Chevy dealership into selling me the 27 cheapest used cars on his lot for $900. I paid for them out of my savings. They were anything but luxury cars. But at least I had a starting inventory I could afford.

My first challenge was finding a suitable lot, inexpensive but well located. I found it on a section of highway on the edge of town. I rented it from the owner for $100 a month. It was cheap, but that's because it was located in lowland. I needed to build the ground up to road level before it was suitable for a car lot.

Without much money to fill in the property, I had an idea: homebuilders in Monroe were digging out basements for new construction. They were hauling the excavated dirt away and dumping it. What if I could convince them not only to give me the dirt, but also to pay me for a place to dump it, on my lot? I contacted several builders, and to my surprise, they agreed. And the money they paid me, $25 a truckload, actually gave me enough cash to buy gravel to put over the fill.

Soon I had my lot upgraded and ready for the chicken coop that would serve as my office.

Yes, a chicken coop. I bought it for $25 from a local farm. I knew the son of the farmer, and the price included delivery. When it arrived, the inside was caked with dried chicken manure as hard as concrete. The smell was almost unbearable. I scraped and cleaned the inside walls for days. I stepped outside only long enough to catch my breath, clear my lungs and grab some fresh air. It was a job that I would never have done for anyone else. But the vision of what the coop would become kept me going. I remember it all so vividly that I can still see and smell it today.

Then I went to work with paint. I remember feeling that with each stroke of the 10 coats I put on the walls, I was a step closer to a new opportunity, even a new life. I laid linoleum on the wood floor. Outside, I used what I had learned while working in the electrical department at Montgomery Ward to install some lighting. I strung bulbs together to hang from four-by-four posts that I had set into the ground around the lot.

I decided to paint the exterior of the coop red and white to catch people's attention from the road. The sign read "Behring Motors." Inside the coop, I had only one lightbulb in the ceiling. But it was my first office. There was no clock to watch, no division of duties, no delegation. I couldn't take off weekends and holidays. It all came down to me, and it was all I could think about.

Suddenly, I was in business. Initially, business was good. I sold my first car, a 1931 Oldsmobile, for $100 just two days after I opened my lot.

But some big challenges came quickly. Within a few months, the rainy season began. And the rain came down. It mixed with the fill I had so cleverly gotten the homebuilders to pay me to dump. I had not put down enough gravel. Before long, the lot was little more than a mud patch. I could not walk without sinking up to my knees in mud. My cars were stuck. The lightpoles tipped; the lights sagged. Would anyone stop to buy a car from me? My competition was not suffering the same way. More than once, I thought of the Chevy dealership, of the warmth of a "real" office and the security of a "real" business.

But that muddy fall turned out to be a bump in the road. Fortunately, there were a few customers who were able to look beyond the appearance of my business to find a good car at a good price, and I was able to make ends meet. Eventually, I had the lot back in shape. More fill dirt. More gravel. Cement bases to secure the light poles. My bank began working with me to buy find better used cars, and I discovered a market that other dealers weren't willing to serve—customers with no credit history. So I began to finance car purchases on my own. I would sell a $500 car to a customer for $75 down and $25 a month until it was paid off. Things were looking up. Pat and I had started to build a house so we could move from our apartment.

Then winter came. I knew it was important to winterize my 50 cars in inventory. But I had just rebuilt my lot and had spent most of my capital. To winterize meant that I needed to buy alcohol or antifreeze, put it in the radiators and run it through the engine of each car. However, I was low on cash and hoped to preserve as much as I could for as long as I could. I put off winterizing my cars.

Bad move.

One morning, I woke up to a bitter cold. An arctic front had rolled into Monroe overnight. The radio said that by evening, the temperature would fall to well below zero. I rushed out to find enough alcohol to winterize my cars. That was no easy task—everyone else in town was buying alcohol for their cars, and there wasn't much in stock at the stores. Each moment I wasted running around to find it was precious, as I had no one to help me get all 50 cars ready by nightfall. The future of Behring Motors and my dreams looked bad.

By the time I was back on the lot, the skies were dark gray. The lot was whipped by a wicked wind, which made being outside almost unbearable. With every car, I had to crawl underneath, my back flat against the frozen gravel, and struggle with cold, dry and often rusted drain cocks. I had no garage. I had no specialized tools. My hands quickly froze beyond feeling. My knuckles become battered and bloodied as my pliers slipped on stubborn bolts. There was little room to move beneath the cars, and when I finally managed to open a drain, ice-cold water poured over my hands and face and soaked my coat and clothes.

I worked as fast as I could. I began with the most expensive cars, just in case I couldn't finish the job before it was too late and before the freeze ruined the remaining cars. By late afternoon, the schools were letting out. I drove to the high school and hired two teenagers to help me. The temperature was below zero. There was not a lot of time left. My fingers were stiff and my back ached. I went home for 10 minutes to change my clothes. But back at the lot, I still could not wear gloves because the bolts and drains that needed loosening were small and required as much nimbleness as my frozen hands could muster. Within an hour, I was soaked again, as water continued to gush out of the drains and flow up my sleeves, over my face and down my neck. But one by one, we worked to drain the radiators and the engines. Then we'd pour in the alcohol and start the cars to circulate it through the engines.

After nightfall, the temperature was 16 degrees below zero.

We had managed to save 25 cars but still had 25 to go. Every movement was painful. As it got colder, many cars would not start, so we couldn't get the alcohol running through the engines. It was slow going. We had to tow some cars a few yards to jump-start them with the clutch.

My mind raced as I scrambled to save my business. My dreams could not end here. I had always believed I'd see them through.

There was no such thing as something that couldn't be done. You'd run into problems, but I believed everything was curable. I realized I needed to plan ahead to survive in business. I should have put more effort into borrowing the money to pay for winterizing. When you are on your own, you have to take care of everything yourself.

In whatever business you are in, there will be problems, so you might as well fix them as they happen because no one else will fix them for you. It takes initiative, sometimes everything you have, to fix the problem.

I climbed under yet another car and then another, struggling to open the drains. I moved more slowly, painfully, pouring in the alcohol, getting the engine started and then moving down the line. Unable to work any longer in the bitter conditions, my hired help went home. I stayed on. The air was so cold that the water draining onto my face and hands and arms and chest froze, despite my body heat. My hands were a mess, red and raw, barely able to grip my tools. The only thing I could feel through the blood was the sting of the alcohol, spilling on me as I worked. By midnight, I realized that I would never get to all the cars in time. Some cars would be lost. It was going to be an expensive lesson in procrastinating and failing to invest money when it was needed. I worked another five hours, to 6 a.m., until I had winterized all but the least expensive cars on the lot. The engines and radiators on the remaining few were already frozen. I would have to sell them for scrap.

I pulled myself from beneath the last car I knew I could save and looked around. I wondered if I could recover from the loss. I turned toward my chicken coop. And that's what it was at that moment—a chicken coop. Not an office. Not the future of Behring Motors. Not even a good investment. The only light was coming from the cheap bulbs I had strung together and hung myself—cheap bulbs dangling over a gravel lot with a bunch of old cars. How could things get any worse?

It started to snow.

We had a few days to move the ruined cars off the lot and get a little cash for them from the junkyard. I sold another few cars to paying customers, which gave me enough working capital for a month. With a little sleep, I went back to work. I was not going to give up. Behring Motors was more than just a business; it was my stake in a brighter future.

That winter, Monroe was hit with one of the biggest snowfalls I can remember. More than three feet of snow fell in a matter of days, and business came to a near standstill. My cars were locked on the lot, buried in snow. The snowplows had piled five- and six-foot banks on either side of the highway, making it impossible for anyone to get in or out of my lot, including me. There were no customers. Again, I was low on money. I was not sure how to proceed, or if I could.

All I knew is that I could not sit by and do nothing. My lot needed to be cleared. Without selling a car or two, I would be in trouble, and the bad weather was settling in. In fact, the only real business moving in Monroe appeared to be the snowplows. No sooner had that thought crossed my mind than I saw an opportunity: I was not the only businessman suffering from bad weather. Everyone in Monroe was. We all needed the same thing, and there was a premium for those who could provide it.

Without enough cash to pay someone to clear my lot, I bartered with a man in town who owned a surplus Army Jeep with four-wheel drive and a plow. I traded him a truck and car. With the Jeep and plow, I went to work clearing my lot and cleaning up my inventory. Still, there were no customers. So Behring Motors diversified. For the next several weeks, I drove the streets of Monroe from 6 a.m. until 11 p.m., looking for any opportunity to make a few dollars by plowing out driveways and business parking lots. It was not part of my original business plan. In fact, it was an accidental opportunity—the result of creative desperation. I realized then, while still in my twenties, that survival, if not success itself, rests in a person's ability to think beyond the current situation.

Too many people, because of their current condition—whether from family challenges, decline of their business or problems with their health—become unable to explore the possibilities that might be right in front of them. Others are simply too complacent or even lazy to see the snow all around them—snow that is killing their business—and realize that that snow may actually be an opportunity just waiting for them to exploit.

In fact, I've learned that within every setback, there's opportunity. You just have to think outside the box to see it. That was true back in Monroe and it's still true today. In any business you go into, you should think, "How can I make opportunity from that setback?" Because someone else always gains from a setback. In a successful business, you should try to be that person.

The weeks of falling snow had threatened to put me into early bankruptcy. It turned into a gift after I traded an old truck and car for a snowplow. With the new perspective of a plowman, I found myself actually hoping for the next snowfall and then the next, knowing that I could resume selling cars in the spring. But until then, I had guaranteed work. I was not going to be sitting alone in my chicken coop worrying about a run of bad luck putting me out of business.

All the time I spent driving the snowplow, I never lost my vision for Behring Motors. If anything, the experience gave me a new perspective and greater energy. It also gave me the chance to meet hundreds of people I had never met before. They hired me to plow their driveways. The relationships we built as I returned with each new snowfall eventually found many of them coming to see me in spring to buy something to put back in their driveways. They not only became customers of my snowplow business but soon looked to me when they wanted to buy a car.

I could close a sale pretty fast, because people wanted to get out of the smell of my office. Looking back, I can only imagine what people must have thought as they passed my little lot, seeing me, in my early twenties, standing ankle deep in mud with customers, looking at used cars. But to me, Behring Motors was never a used car lot. It was the first realization of my dreams. It was freedom, a destination and a voyage. I was making my own decisions. Success or failure would be my responsibility. Behring Motors was more than a livelihood. It was a school where I continued to learn principles that would allow me to build my business.

I made some mistakes, largely due to my own greed. One I still regret, from my days as a Hudson salesman, was inflating the price of a junk car I sold to a kid who I took as an easy mark. The car actually belonged to a friend of mine, and, as a favor to him, I made the sale through the dealership, with the owner's permission. The sale was easy—too easy. The finance company was happy to make the loan, because the dealership guaranteed it. But when the kid didn't make his monthly payments—he probably never intended to—the finance company repossessed the car. It was in terrible shape, half wrecked. I could have stuck the dealer with the mess, but I didn't, paying the finance company myself. (The dealer was a nice guy who had been trying to help me and had done my friend a favor.) As they said in Monroe, "You feed the pigs, but you send the hogs to market." My greed butchered my personal finances.

I soon realized that successful transactions are win-win and that strong financial foundations are built slowly, and built to last. I learned to be much more careful in sales. I still had to sell junk cars from time to time, but I sold them at junk prices, not inflated ones. I learned you can't sell someone something for more than he or she can afford. The truth is that no one is ever successful if he takes advantage of people. A deal has to be fair for all parties. You can't take advantage of someone just because they don't know better.

That philosophy turned out to be good for business. Because I treated people fairly, the word got out in the community that I was a good person to deal with.

My client base was growing. With warmer weather, I was able to move my inventory and invest in better cars. My work through the winter, and my ability to save the business, improved my reputation and my credibility with the bank. I was now a trusted client. Soon, the bank let me borrow money against the finer used cars I purchased for inventory. At the time, consumer interest rates were high, at double digits. But my banker, Roland Blaha, was willing to lend me money at 6 percent. He taught me the awesome potential of financing.

My favorable bank relationship allowed me to enter the finance business. I'd sell my cars and finance them at a market interest rate and repay the bank at its lower "best customer" rate. Soon, I found that I could make more money through financing than by selling. It was also beneficial for my customers, many of whom couldn't afford to buy a car outright or were struggling with bad credit.

Again, Roland's faith in me paid dividends, as he and the bank backed all of my loans. It was the same faith he had demonstrated years earlier when, for no apparent reason, he had allowed me at 17 to sign the financing for my own car. Most people could not take out a car loan until they were 21. But for some reason Roland believed in me. He was willing to finance anything I proposed, and I often wonder where I would be today had he not been so willing to take the risks he did. In fact, there were times when he brought the ideas to me. He convinced me some years later to build the first apartments in Monroe, a small number of units that he taught me how to secure with federal guarantees.

With Roland's support, I gradually learned that success comes through seeing how much you can give the consumer for his money, not from worrying about how much of his money you can get.

Behring Motors grew faster than anyone could have predicted. People knew they would pay a fair price and that I would look out for them and provide affordable financing. That financing, in turn, provided something new and wonderful for me: the stability of recurring income. Every month, hundreds of people would sit down and write checks to Behring Motors. That steady income allowed me to take my next step.

I wanted to open a second location. I invited my father-in-law, H.W. "Budd" Riffle, to join the expanding business. Budd was a colorful and warm personality who loved music and dancing. He was a devoted father and had actually been a golfing friend of mine before I began dating his daughter. In Monroe, he had built a career as an advertising manager at the local newspaper. But like me, he wanted to be his own boss and build his own future.

With Behring Motors established, we opened Ken-Budd Used Car Sales on the other side of town. Budd was a natural with customers, as well as a good partner. Our solid customer relationships led to further business development, and before long we were moving into new cars, including foreign imports. We believed in aggressive sales tactics, advertising and participating in community organizations.

Meanwhile, the money I was earning by moving better inventory and providing financing allowed me to relocate Behring Motors from my disadvantaged outdoor location to a lot in town with a garage. It was the old Studebaker dealership, which had gone out of business.

I rented it month to month. I hired my first salesmen, Dick Bienema, my friend from high school who was back from the Coast Guard. Dick and I worked hard, seven days a week, from 8 in the morning until 11 at night. Our financing operation grew to include auto insurance.

Sales were so strong that within a few years, Ford Motors contacted me about opening the first Lincoln-Mercury dealership in Monroe. We tried to lease the Studebaker building for it, but the owner would not rent it to us long-term. Again, I had to come up with a creative solution to a problem. Through my bank, I found a farmer who would lend me enough money to buy the material for the garage. Luckily, I found a lot on the edge of town and was able to talk Dick Bienema and my other employees into doing the labor to build the garage while I made enough money selling cars to maintain their salaries. We went to auction and bid on equipment to use for construction. Although it was an ambitious plan, somehow we completed the garage and opened for business in less than a year.

In 1953, Behring Motors became Behring Lincoln-Mercury, and our decision paid off. Within two years, we were exceeding our quota of new car sales by more than 800 percent. One month, we outsold the combined total sales of the six Chevrolet and four Ford dealerships in the county. We were using every form of promotion we could think of. We announced a contest: whoever stood in a line the longest would win a $300 used car. It was summer; there were a lot of flies. The people standing in line got to see all of our cars, and the people driving by on the highway saw all the people standing in line. It was a great public relations stunt that made the local newspaper. Someone stood there for five days to win that car.

We were known as the "crazy people." We were horse traders—literally. We took riding horses, motorcycles, milk machines—even watches—in trade. Our pitch was that if customers could come up with enough value in a trade-in to make a down payment, we would finance the rest of the purchase. Of course, we took cash for down payments, too.

Other dealers didn't like our tactics very much because in their eyes, we weren't quite legitimate. We felt we were just being innovative. Dealerships were largely family businesses back then; sons took over from their fathers and did exactly what was done before. We came in and blew them out of the water. We held high-profile promotions. We started the discounting and everyone had to follow.

We were open until 11 p.m. each day and open on Sundays. Every other dealer closed at 6 p.m. and on Sundays. For us, it was a seven-day-a-week job. The only day we closed was Christmas. It proved once again to me that the harder you work, the more fortunate you are.

About then, I had another close call with my life. The first had been that childhood car accident. This time, I almost died because of my love of sports and speed. My friends and I liked to build small speedboats and race them on local lakes. One day in 1954, I was working on a boat in our service garage. I didn't know it, but gasoline fumes were building up under the hood. When I climbed into the seat and tested the starter, BOOM, the boat exploded. I don't remember anything about it. But my friends said the explosion threw me 100 yards in a ball of flame. The blast also blew out two plate glass windows in the showroom. I was burned over more than 80 percent of my body. It was very painful. Fortunately, there was a doctor nearby. He made me immediately drink salt water, which helped protect my burned skin. I was in the hospital only two or three days. When I walked back into work, our bookkeeper almost passed out. I did not look good.

I had always felt that guardian angels watched over me. This was the second time I had cheated death. Higher powers wanted to keep me around for some purpose.

Part II

Better

Chapter 4:
THE SUNSHINE STATE

Behold the turtle. He makes progress
only when he sticks his neck out.

James Bryant Conant

Three years after starting Behring Lincoln-Mercury, I was a
27-year-old making $50,000 a year and I had a million dollars in
assets. Monroe was getting smaller. I looked around and became
aware that some people still had more than I did. I wasn't satisfied.
I was tired of the auto business after a decade of selling cars.

My father-in-law, Budd, had retired from our used car company
three years earlier. He made retired life look very attractive. Both he
and I had become golf nuts, and I was intrigued by the prospect of a
quiet life dedicated to perfecting my game. Perhaps this was the
chance. In 1956, I decided to sell my dealership to Dick Bienema
and Lloyd Siedschlag, another friend I had convinced to join the
business. I kept only the finance operation and the building. I also
still owned rental apartments. With income from investments and
the sale of the dealership, I had more than enough money to retire in

Florida, and at that moment, that's what I thought I might do. In the late 1940s, we had vacationed there. Coming from Wisconsin, where winter temperatures hit 30 degrees below, the sunshine and beaches of Florida seemed like paradise.

I also knew there was opportunity in the Sunshine State. Ford had approached me about opening another Lincoln-Mercury dealership in Miami, and a fellow auto dealer had recommended Fort Lauderdale, an up-and-coming city north of Miami. To check things out, I sent one of my most enterprising employees, Bob Trachsel, down to explore the state. I trusted Bob. He was industrious and loyal. Like most of those who joined my team, he had come from poverty; he began to work at a filling station as soon as he was old enough. Tall and skinny, Bob was five years younger than I was. I had hired him right out of high school. More than anything, he was dependable, and I took his recommendation. After some looking around, Bob agreed there might be good opportunities in Fort Lauderdale.

It didn't take me long to realize how perceptive Bob had been. Fort Lauderdale had a small community of professionals shaping its future. One was a visionary land developer, Jim Hunt, the head of Coral Ridge Properties. He had created the Galt Ocean Mile, among other premium developments. Jim was the first big promoter of expensive land and lots, and though we would not become friends until some years later, I admired him from a distance. I was impressed by his prominence in Fort Lauderdale's business community as well as his strength and ability to manage conditions around him. He was a heavyset man with a strong personality. He later give me some valuable advice as I built my second career in real estate: "Never take both hands off the pump," he said. "As an entrepreneur, you need to be on constant lookout for opportunity, and that will involve risk. But you minimize those risks by keeping one hand on the pump that's producing for you."

But in the summer of 1956, I honestly didn't know what I was going to do with the rest of my life when I moved my family to Fort Lauderdale. By then, we had had the first three of our five sons. We sold our house in Monroe with all the furnishings. Pat sat silently next to me in the front seat of our Lincoln, holding nine-month-old David on her lap. Michael and Tom, ages five and three, played and wrestled and colored in the back. Pat was supportive of our new adventure. Her silence didn't mean she was concerned about our decision to move. Rather, I think it showed her adaptable nature. This makes her not only the best wife in the world, but perhaps the only woman who would ever put up with me. She has always trusted my instincts. Pat and I moved our family into a rented duplex and enrolled Michael in first grade at Wilton Manors public school. I began reaching out to businessmen in the community and started to search for a suitable lot on which to build a home. After I found one, I worked with an architect to design a luxurious model in the $30,000 range, a substantial investment for the time. But before it was completed, a few people offered me almost $40,000 for the property.

I had been used to making $200 and $300s profit on an automobile. Believe me, the offers on our new house got my attention. I was intrigued by the prospect of making almost $10,000 in profit on the sale of a single home. I gave in and began to build a second home in the same price range. Again, I was offered thousands more than I had invested. I sold it and began a third home. This, too, went for a good profit, and I finally realized that a pattern had been established. I had accidentally become a homebuilder.

With Bob Trachsel at my side, I opened Behring Construction Company and moved my parents to Florida. My father went to work for me as a carpenter. We began by building on five lots and selling properties in the $18,000 to $25,000 price range. They went quickly, and I decided to expand. I took in partners to pursue larger projects. We were a hardworking group with a family atmosphere. My father enjoyed getting out with the laborers every day, pounding nails and hanging sheetrock. My mother would make large doughnuts for the crews. In the expansion, I was able to bring more friends down from Wisconsin, including Dan Poff, who had built the apartments in Monroe for me. Dan was an honest and hardworking contractor willing to take a risk. Along with Dan, I convinced Dick Bienema to move south.

It was a good team. Our first major development included 350 units that we turned into waterfront properties by digging canals and building up the land around them. Taking another lesson from Jim Hunt, who could have put P.T. Barnum to shame, I learned to bang the drum loudly. I hired a public relations firm and held major media events to establish the reputation of our homes and land development. Beyond getting a fair markup on the price of a home, the real money came by increasing the value of the land. That was one part vision, one part labor and one part showmanship. The art was in getting others to see its value the way you did. In the beginning, that wasn't easy; much of the land was swampy and had to be dredged and built up. Showmanship attracted investors, and I was soon surrounded by a group of blue-chip partners. We'd split our profits 50-50.

We were also building condominiums, some of the first in the nation. But some of my customers kept telling me that what they really preferred was a single-family home on its own lot with the benefits of condo living—maintenance handled by an association for a fee, community gathering places and more.

So we went to work. We bought 13 acres west of Fort Lauderdale. I named the planned development Tamarac. (The name was similar to the name of a country club I belonged to.) My attorney, Bill Morse, was confident and well connected. He and his wife were big players in state politics. His firm was highly regarded in Tallahassee, the capital. I had hired him to help me with zoning issues and to develop the relatively new concepts of condominiums and land leases. But Bill soon had me involved in politics, supporting candidates like Bud Dickenson, who went on to help establish the Florida Council of 100—a group of business, community and political leaders that I joined.

Bill's firm was helping one candidate for a state senate campaign. In the politics of the old days, I agreed to support him if he would help me in Tallahassee if he won. He did. Once in office, he helped me secure a city charter for Tamarac through the state legislature. It was controversial—we won a charter for 13 acres of raw land. Until then, charters went to communities that were already built out.

This was 1962. On March 3 of the following year, we held the grand opening of Tamarac, the first city in the United States to offer yard mowing, hedge trimming, exterior painting, roof cleaning and year-round recreational programs with a full-time recreational director as a service of the city. It was a unique concept; it had never been done before. We catered to people 55 and older. Our homes were priced at $8,990 to $12,990. It was a popular concept, and soon we were buying land west of the city, expanding the community to 10,000 acres in all. I controlled the charter, so I made Bill Morse mayor. Today, Tamarac has about 60,000 residents.

We based our communities on the idea that retirees wanted a chance to meet and make friends with people like themselves who were moving from their hometowns to Florida. In each area, we constructed 250 homes and a clubhouse, swimming pool, shuffleboard and other recreational amenities. We started many clubhouse activities such as bingo, dancing and barbecues that made each common area a welcome gathering place. Residents no longer needed to worry about outside maintenance, as it was all included in a $23-per-month fee to the city.

It was a big success. "Adult Leisure Living Idea Hits the Jackpot" was the headline in the local paper three years after we broke ground. But it also was one of the first times that I had an inkling of a greater purpose in life. Not only was Tamarac good business, it was something good. We gave people freedom and friendship—at a price they could afford. We created a way of life for them. Now, rather than sitting around in houses waiting to die, retired people could move to Florida to a nice home. They would not have to worry about property maintenance and upkeep and could enjoy a retirement full of fun and activities. My neighborhoods became competitive; residents often approached me to tell me that theirs was the best and most active. And I never raised prices much because I wanted to give this way of life to as many people as possible. It was a lifestyle that was no longer reserved for the wealthy alone.

I got a lot of satisfaction out of it all. I was the "father of the city." I umpired the softball games between neighborhoods. On New Year's Eve, I'd visit every clubhouse to greet the residents. They'd play "Hail to the Chief" when I walked in.

Tamarac's growth brought banks, shopping centers, hospitals, golf courses and everything needed for a comfortable life. Later, the original houses sold for as much as $175,000. The area looks as good today as the day we built it because of the maintenance and the pride the residents have in their community.

Pat and I built our home in the Woodlands, an exclusive country club community I developed in Tamarac. It featured two 18-hole championship golf courses designed by Robert Von Hagge and a 58,000-foot clubhouse. Single-family residences ranged from $30,000 to $55,000 in the 640-acre community. It was soon dubbed "Broward's Fashionable West End."

When I turned 40 in 1968, Pat and my friends threw me one heck of a party. The antics were so outrageous that they made the *Miami Herald*. The invitations carried an illustration of me dressed only in a diaper and sitting on top of the world. The cover of the invitation read, "Life begins at 40." The inside copy continued,

"Friends of Ken Behring hope to prove this to him." They did that at a rollicking celebration that began at noon and did not end until well into the next day. The bash took place at the Woodlands, where every model home was opened and featured a bar based on a different theme. All homes served barbecued boar, while four bands played continuously for the three or four thousand people who attended the event.

Our financial success in Tamarac was largely due to our purchase of large tracts of land for future development. I had strong people handling land purchased from farmers in the area. Dick Anderson, my marketing manager, sealed a deal for a tract of 1,380 acres that paved the way for the first large expansion of Tamarac. It provided space for a shopping center, golf courses, 1,750 retirement homes and woodlands. It also included a high-end area with two golf courses and expensive villas and homes. Dick was also in charge of selling all commercial land and recreation leases. Chuck Langston, a former baseball player, helped purchase a tract of 5,000 acres that provided the land for the rest of Tamarac. He also found a 3,500-acre tract west of Palm Beach. We built Boca West, a retirement area, there. He also was responsible for our land purchases in St. Petersburg and Lake Tarpon in northwest Florida.

These acquisitions and the increases in the value of our land holdings were the reason we could go public in 1969 and eventually sell the corporation to Cerro Corporation in 1972. As we continued to build Tamarac, we also developed some of the most beautiful and prestigious communities in the state—Royal Palm Isles, Cherry Creek Estates and Gramercy Park in the Coral Ridge Country Club. By 1972, we'd also built hundreds of custom homes and established ourselves as the largest builder in Florida and the 10th largest in the nation.

In Tamarac, Pat blossomed, becoming a community leader in her own right. She joined a number of service organizations, hosting fundraisers and getting actively involved in our children's schools. She was asked to join Beaux Arts, an organization that raised funds for the Fort Lauderdale Museum of Art, and served as chair of the "April in Paris" Easter Lily Ball. She learned how to drive. Pat took on the role of caretaker and provider in the social relationships we enjoyed. She befriended the wives of my partners and served as emotional ambassador to my employees. Everything whirled around us, but Pat was the rock. She held our family together. She made sure we attended the boys' school events and did our part to support community and academic programs.

One successful program we started in Florida was the Behring Outstanding Teacher Award at Pine Crest School, the private school in Fort Lauderdale that our kids attended. We began the program in 1973. It required faculty, administrators and students to vote for three outstanding teachers at the end of the school year. We gave $5,000 to each of those teachers. They were honored at an assembly and featured in the local news. It was an exciting time when the school named the new teachers. But what I found fascinating was that every year the faculty, administrators and students agreed on the winning teachers. It was as if each year, like clockwork, three teachers would distinguish themselves above the rest and be identified unanimously in a private ballot by the three voting blocs. Through the years, Pat has stayed in touch with many of the recipients of the Outstanding Teacher Award. We are proud of their accomplishments and the lives they have powerfully influenced as educators and school leaders.

I also found purpose in this awards program. The goal was to motivate the best. We feel we did. But we also enjoyed it because we were accomplishing much more for the school than the value of the money we donated to the program. There was purpose to our giving. After the boys graduated from Pine Crest, the Behring Awards ended. But Pat and I established an endowment at the school that provided ongoing grants to teachers for continuing education.

Pine Crest provided our children with strong academic programs and offered them a wonderful environment. David, our third son, excelled in academics and on the football field. At 5 feet 10 inches and 185 pounds, he became the leading all-time single-season ground gainer in the history of Broward County football, carrying the ball 189 times during the regular season for a total of 1,396 yards. He shattered the old record of 1,246 yards and set individual rushing records in nine games his senior year. In the 10th game, playing on a badly swollen ankle, he led the Pine Crest Panthers to a 6-0 win over Dade Christian by scoring the only touchdown and rushing more than 100 yards. It gave Pine Crest its first undefeated season and district title. Including post-season play that year, David racked up 1,487 yards on 197 carries and scored 12 touchdowns, averaging 7.5 yards per carry.

The fact that I remember these statistics so many years later is a testament to how proud I was of him, as I am of all my sons. Jeff, our fourth son, earned an unprecedented 12 major varsity sports letters. He was a good student and courageously competitive in everything he did. He was by far the most athletic in the family, and we were all envious of his ability to quickly master almost any sport.

As a family, we enjoyed fishing, often traveling into the Arctic Circle to catch trout in the Great Slave and Great Bear Lakes and going after black marlin and sailfish off the coast of Panama. On several occasions, we visited Coiba, a Panamanian prison island. The fishing was great. The waters were home to a submerged island with dozens of different classes of sport fish. In a single day, we caught 28 different varieties. At night, we played volleyball with the inmates and locals, who told us tales of prison life and attempted escapes from the island.

One day, we were fishing in an area inhabited by shark and orca. Jeff lost his grip on the rod as he cast his line. Instinctively, he dove into the shark- and orca-infested water to retrieve the rod and reel. David grabbed him before sharks could attack.

"What are you doing?" he screamed at his wet younger brother. "The sharks could have killed you."

"The sharks or Dad," Jeff answered. "And I figured I had a better chance with the sharks."

It's not that I was a difficult father. But I was as demanding as I was proud. The boys worked hard and played hard at baseball, football, track and tennis. As they grew, each son's unique talents and personalities emerged. They were smart. Michael, our first son, was a gifted artist, with a creative temperament and an interest in music. Tom, our second son, fell in love with books, psychology, philosophy and baseball, and I came to appreciate his thoughtful nature. Perhaps of all the boys, Tom was the most like Pat—a gentle teddy bear, soft-spoken and loved by his nephews and nieces. Scott, our fifth son, was called to the great outdoors and was never one to engage in the conventional life. He played football, lacrosse and wrestled at Pine Crest. Like Tom, he was kind and sensitive, earnest in his relationships and quick to make a friend. In all, the boys were a tribute to Pat and her gift at motherhood. I was a father from the old school, focused on building the business and emotionally distant. My love was demonstrated more than it was expressed. Showing love was, and remains, difficult. I probably inherited that from my father, just as he inherited it from his. It was compounded by the fact that I worked 15-hour days, seven days a week. I am grateful that Pat was—and remains—so supportive of our children.

In January 1969, the Miami Herald published a feature article about Pat. It was headlined, "She's Gracious Amid Wealth." The story quotes Pat as saying, "I enjoy the excitement of living with a man who is becoming well-known." The article continues:

That statement is as close as Pat Behring will get to preten-

tiousness. A woman who describes herself as an introvert, Mrs. Behring is exceedingly gracious. She jumps to offer coffee and her mother-in-law's homemade fruitcake. She realizes instinctively the needs of others, works to put her guests at ease. She succeeds.

Behring Properties, her husband's company, has an estimated net worth of between $15 and $20 million. But it's people, not money, that matter to Mrs. Behring.

"You have to be tolerant of your husband's time. You have to be willing to share with his business," she said, adding, "When I need him, he's there."

"He's the head of the home, although the responsibility for everyday things falls on me.... I don't think I could ever find a more exciting man."

Pat was, and continues to be, gracious. The Herald story may appear dated in relation to today's attitudes, but there's no question that her support provided the foundation I needed to build our career. Business did not end at the front door, and Pat never hesitated to help me in whatever venture I was pursuing. Our Woodlands home was filled with guests and galas and even historic press conferences.

One of most exciting press events was with the legendary entertainer Jackie Gleason. I met Gleason through a friend. Bob von Hagge worked with Gleason on golf courses. Bob suggested I hire Gleason's Miami public relations man. Soon I had met Jackie and we were in business together.

Gleason and I planned to build the most magnificent golf courses in the world on a major development, with luxury homes. The centerpiece of the six-course complex, to be designed by Bob, would be a 7,300-yard championship course known as "The Great One"—Gleason's nickname. We planned to host a Professional Golfers' Association event there, "Nonpareil"—at $300,000, the richest cup on the tour. Our plans included a three-tiered stadium and room for 100,000 spectators on the course. Permanent television towers on each hole would provide perfect network coverage for all tournaments.

We announced the project in 1969. According to Jackie, it even had the blessing of President Richard Nixon. Attending the media event were Colin Brown, president and chairman of National Gypsum; his vice president of corporate affairs, William Duncan; Judge John P. Lomenzo, a good friend of mine and secretary of state of New York; executives from 3M; and Bob von Hagge and his wife, Greta, one of the beautiful June Taylor dancers who opened Gleason's show every week with his signature line, "And away we go!"

"We will not be topped!" The Great One bellowed to the press.

"If someone offers to match or beat our purse, we will up the ante so that the 'Nonpareil' will be the richest tourney in history. I've found plenty of men with great ideas and with guts, but never before have I found one who also has the cabbage," he said, complimenting me.

He then told reporters that the first tournament was already in planning, with 3M as the sponsor. His network, CBS, would broadcast the five-day event, he said.

Not only was Gleason "The Great One," he was also the great improviser. He held court in our home, painting a vivid picture of the future. I stood next to him, nervously calculating the time and money involved in the venture, not to mention the cost of working with Jackie Gleason, who had only one way of doing things—his way. The project would cost more than half a billion dollars. It would cover 5,000 acres of prime land between Fort Lauderdale and Pompano Beach. It would require zoning, architectural designs, new roads and the creation of an island inaccessible to automobile traffic, where Jackie intended to have his palace overlooking the ninth, 16th, 17th and 18th holes. It would require us to move a million and a half cubic yards of earth. And here he was, not only locking down the tel- evision rights of the first tournament, but committing that the project would be completed by the end of the following year.

And away we go.

In the end, Gleason and I went our separate ways. We realized we wouldn't be able to complete the project. In the best of show business terms, you could say that we had "creative differences." Jackie wanted a showcase for his home, his talent and his life lived large in every sense of the term. I simply wanted to make money. It was not long before we realized that we could not have it both ways. We quietly dropped the venture six months after the press conference.

Unlike Gleason, I was pragmatic about land development and the construction business. I had weathered economic slumps and worked through labor shortages. I'd seen my business turned upside down by price spikes in building materials. I'd suffered attacks from politicians trying to make an issue out of zoning ordinances and land leases. Through it all, I had proved that I could make things work. I could stand up to Gleason and his desire to build an adult Disney World. We parted as friends. Besides, I had become interested in factory-produced housing, and that began to take up more of my time.

We had a problem in the building business. In 1968, lumber prices rose 33 percent, particularly for plywood and softwood framing lumber. National housing starts were projected to hit 1.5 million that year, far short of need. The industry was plagued by a shortage of qualified craftsmen. Florida was in a recession. The solution to these challenges, I believed, was steel-framed factory-built homes. Mine would be as beautiful as traditional homes, but they could be built in a factory and assembled on a lot in three pieces at a much lower cost. Total assembly time would be one hour.

I still believe it was a good idea. We'd be able to build houses in much higher quantities to meet demand. We'd get around labor problems to stabilize the costs of building. And we'd standardize everything, with the exception of consumer preferences in colors, façade, models and amenities.

I took time to educate myself on the prefabricated housing market. I learned that that no one was producing a quality product. I assembled a team to meet the challenge I presented: build a perfect home that could be mass-produced in a controlled factory environment and assembled quickly but permanently on a lot, while providing all the beauty and options available in traditional construction. I asked Bill Brangham, my executive vice president at the Behring Corporation, to lead the group. Bill was gifted at sales and marketing and possessed good insight into consumer attitudes.

George Smith, vice president of Behring Properties, oversaw the engineering and materials management. I had hired him away from General Electric along with several other GE alumni. Working with John Evans, our project architect, and Evan Morton, project engineer, George put together the infrastructure blueprint for what we called Modiflex Homes. The venture grabbed media attention from the day we announced it in May 1969.

We constructed the first prototype on a lot in Tamarac. It generated so much interest that we had to build a wall to keep people out. Some of them were coming from outside the country to see what we were doing. Top materials and steel frames made our homes more durable than traditional wood homes. To make them attractive, we developed five different models. Each could be assembled in three pieces on a prepoured concrete foundation with plumbing and electrical hookups. We transported each one from factory to lot on three flatbed trailers. One truck would carry the bedroom wing; another, the living room section; and the third a wet wing, containing bathrooms, utility room, kitchen and dining room. Each section would be hoisted from the flatbed by a giant crane and bolted to the foundation by cast-in-steel inserts. When the sections were in place and fastened to each other with steel bolts, the roof would be lowered into position and workmen would connect the plumbing and electricity.

Along with the five models, we offered over 150 variations on the exterior. At the end of assembly, a Modiflex Home—though less expensive to build and more durable in construction—would look no different from a traditional home next door. With assembly-line efficiency, we could sell units and lots from $12,000 to $17,000 and promise buyers that they could be in their new homes within a week. Convinced of our vision, we built the factory in Tamarac. It was a 250,000-square-foot facility that cost more than $4 million.

The venture created international buzz. Government officials, economists, industrialists and builders came from as far away as Japan to tour our facility. Many observers were interested in joint venturing with us to build Modiflex Homes in their countries. We set up an educational center to meet the demands of the curious, with maps, color photographs, diagrams and models. In a three-month period, we had more than 250,000 visitors. Even the Shah of Iran sent a representative to learn about what we were doing.

The timing was right. In Washington, Congress was calling for solutions to the housing shortage. In a speech, Sen. Harrison A. Williams, a member of the Senate Housing Committee, challenged Americans to "devote the same energy and talent that enabled us to win the race to the moon to home building." Speaking to the National Housing Center Council, which was made up of manufacturer members of the National Association of Home Builders, Williams said, "In recent years, there has been much rhetoric about a missile gap or space gap followed by huge expenditures for our military and space programs…. It's time we focused our attention on the housing gap." Earlier, the Commerce Department had predicted that within a few years, the United States would lag far behind other countries in housing its people. It said that the best-housed people in the world would be living in the Soviet Union.

Senator Williams quoted the department and said, "If a Pentagon general said the same thing about missiles, there would be an enormous clamor for a multi-billion-dollar crash program.... It is a national disgrace that the United States is falling far behind other nations in providing better housing. Last year, the United States built 7.69 new housing units per 1,000 residents. By way of contrast, Sweden built 13.43 units per 1,000, Japan built 11.89, the Soviet Union built 9.80, the Netherlands built 9.63 and France built 8.32."

For a while, it appeared not only that we had met the marketing needs of consumers, but that we were onto something of tremendous importance to American public policy. We offered an attractive, efficient and cost-effective answer to meeting the nation's growing housing needs. One popular magazine put a Modiflex Home on its cover and proclaimed, "Assembly Line Homes: An Important New Trend in Housing." My small company had grown from a handful of close friends to more than 700 employees.

Another magazine wrote that the ideas coming from the Behring Corporation were the "fountainhead of most significant developments." Whether intentional or not, the reference to the book by libertarian economist and philosopher Ayn Rand would prove fitting for Modiflex Homes. Rand's book *The Fountainhead* is about a visionary architect who creates revolutionary buildings that solve serious social problems. But his work is undone by government bureaucracies, unions, rivals and traditionalists. It was the perfect metaphor for our new company. As word spread about the popularity of Modiflex Homes, so did opposition.

First, the carpenters' union came out against us. It suggested that Modiflex Homes would undermine the security of its members and even destroy its organization. That didn't deter us. We were using highly skilled labor in our factory and could weather the challenge. But soon, the union solicited and gained support from the Teamsters union, a group that could not be broken. Suddenly, truckers would not transport our homes from factory to lot. Next, our opponents launched a major lobbying effort against us in state legislatures and city halls. What we were doing, they charged, was risky. We were challenging conventional thinking and the long history of traditional homebuilding, perhaps even undermining the economy. Under pressure from special interest groups, cities and towns began delaying and even denying zoning for our homes. Soon it began to taking us longer to get a government permit than to build the home. New battles emerged every day.

In *The Fountainhead,* the hero/architect retreats in the end and destroys his visionary creations. I was determined to press forward.

But we had miscalculated. Suddenly, our best workers began leaving the factory. They could earn $2 an hour more in construction jobs in the field. Hoping to keep our costs down, I had talked the union into working for us for a rate that now appeared too low. I had not anticipated the possible consequences. When I offered to increase workers' wages, their union said, "No way. That's the rate you wanted. That's the rate you get." The union's goal was to protect its members working on construction sites. Before long, I could not recruit the quality people who could do the job right. I learned a valuable lesson.

The apparent solution to our problem came from the outside. With the success of the homebuilding business, our land leases and our holdings in Tamarac (including shopping centers, recreational and maintenance contracts, increasingly valuable property and a city charter itself), several large companies were interested in acquiring the Behring Corporation. I began to consider offers seriously. I was intrigued by the possibility that for the first time in my life, I wouldn't have to worry about money or managing anything. No more juggling payroll and payables, keeping my company together on perception and the good fortune of not having banks call my loans. I could see freedom, but I was also worried about what would come next if I sold out.

Still, companies willing to pay me more than I ever imagined were courting me. My team and I had created something of value, and I felt good about that. I entertained offers from Bethlehem Steel, Dupont, Chrysler and National Gypsum. The closest I came to selling was entering a tentative deal with National Gypsum for $30 million in stock. However, it required me to stay and help run the company I was selling. And when I traveled to the corporation's headquarters in upstate New York, I was shocked. There were layers of management, emotionless bureaucrats, countless meetings—all of the things I dreaded about big business. I considered calling off the deal.

By this time, Jim Hunt had become a good friend. He was the godfather of land development and property management in Fort Lauderdale. He had become something of a mentor, first telling me never to take both hands off the pump, then teaching me by example how to create buzz to promote sales and increase the value of land.

As I was struggling with my decision, he shared with me his regret for having sold his beloved Coral Ridge Properties to Westing-house Corporation two years earlier. Not long after the transaction, he invited me to lunch. Sitting across the table as glum as Woody Allen, he expressed his unhappiness. "They made me rich," he said. "And I have an office. But it has bars around it. Every once in a while, they come in with a stick and poke me to see if I'll growl." Once supreme ruler of his own domain, Jim had been stripped of his motivation. He made it clear to me that the measure of success in business sometimes has little to do with making money. "Everything is run by committee," he told me. "No one takes risks. The emotion is gone." Westinghouse had even installed the man who served as

Jim's number two at Coral Ridge Properties as Jim's boss.

I took his advice to heart. I told National Gypsum I would not enter into a formal contract. Instead, I took the greater risk and asked the Oppenheimer Company on Wall Street to take me public. Working with a couple of bright young advisors, including Tom Seward and Henry Silverman, we merged six of the 30-plus companies I owned—including Modiflex Homes, the city charter of Tamarac, land and my home-building business—into one company to be listed on the American Stock Exchange. We sold a million shares at $16.50 a share. I retained about five million shares. In the first few days of trading, the stock shot up to $30 a share. That amount of money and my sudden wealth—I was worth $150 million on paper—was almost inconceivable to me.

My mother, thankfully, was around to keep me grounded. I had given her shares in my company before the public offering. Her question to me was, "What am I supposed to do with them?"

"You keep them," I answered. "And after the company goes public and the value of the shares increase, you sell them." "Why?"

"To make money."

"How do I make money?" "By selling the shares."

"What do I have to do?" Her question was filled with suspicion. I answered as simply as I could. "You just have to sell the shares."

"Do I have to attend meetings?" "No."

"Do I have to do anything for anyone?"

"No, you hold the shares and then sell them." "And they give me the money, just like that?" "Exactly."

She slid the stock certificate back across my desk. "Doesn't seem right."

Despite the opportunities and money I provided them, my parents refused to spend what I gave them to enjoy the finer things in life. After they were gone, I found thousands of dollars hidden in their mattresses—along with my football clippings. I wish I had known they saved those clippings when they were alive. If only my parents had been able to share them with me, I would have known how much they really cared.

As for my newfound wealth, I now had a large bank account. But before long, that would not be enough for me—again.

Chapter 5:
A PLACE CALLED BLACKHAWK

Far better to dare mighty things, to win glorious
triumphs, even though checkered by failure, than
to rank with those poor spirits who neither enjoy
much, nor suffer much because they live in the
great twilight that knows not victory nor defeat.

Theodore Roosevelt

If there's a pattern to my life, it's that I do something new about
every 10 years. In the 1950s, it was the automobile business. In the
1960s, I developed land in Florida. By the end of that decade, I was
manufacturing preconstructed homes.

The activities of one period always overlapped. But one cycle
was becoming certain: about every decade, I would become restless
and need to make a major change in my life. I believe every life
comes with the possibility of great adventure and that new pursuits
will keep the adventure alive, the mind sharp and boredom at bay.
I sometimes follow one opportunity to another, but I often set out to
make a wholesale change—a new environment, a new purpose, new
discoveries and new friends.

That was the case in 1972.

I sold my company that year to Cerro Corporation, a major

copper company that was diversifying and owned Leadership Housing, the division that would run the Behring Corporation. After the
deal, I had about $50 million in net worth. I had decided I didn't like
run- ning a public company after all. I didn't like the restrictions
that came with being public, such as government filings and constant reports to shareholders. My 10 years was up again, this time
with the building business in Florida. With the sale of my company,
I had achieved the American Dream. But where to go and what to do
next?

I decided to take a month off to think about it. I planned to take
my family and mother to Europe for a needed rest. I wanted to
reward everyone for putting up with me while I was under the pressure of selling my company. My mother helped ease the pressure
with a funny, but typical, incident.

I sent the family ahead to Switzerland as I went to New York to
finish some business. I always stayed at the Waldorf Towers. My
mother met me there. My secretary accompanied her to New York
and was to bring my mother up to my suite on the 30th floor. She had
never been in an elevator; she refused to enter it, saying she would
walk up 30 stories. I rode down to the lobby and pulled her into the
elevator. She held her hands over her eyes on the way up.

It was evening and we were flying to Switzerland the following
day. I had to leave early for a meeting, so I asked her what she wanted for breakfast the next morning. I told her it would be brought to
her room. She said she wanted coffee, eggs, bacon and toast.

The next day, when I returned to the hotel after my meetings, the
bellman told me there had been a problem. Apparently, when room
service delivered my mother her breakfast, she had refused to sign
for it. "I am not going to let you rob my son!" she told the waiter.

"All you had to do is sign," I told her. "You didn't have to pay."
"I could not eat food that expensive," she said.

After we returned from Europe, I began to explore new possibilities. I traveled to Asia to consult and look at some of the dynamic growth occurring in the Pacific Rim. One morning when I was in Tokyo, the phone rang in my hotel room. It was Bruce Devlin, a golf course architect I had worked with in Florida to build 10 courses. He was calling from the States. Even with the phone connection fading in and out, I could hear excitement in Bruce's voice.

"On your way back to Florida, you need to stop in California," Bruce said. "I think there's something here you'll be interested to see."

"What do you have?" I asked.

"I don't want to tell you over the telephone. I want you to see it for yourself."

I trusted Bruce. He knew how to spot an opportunity, and I was interested. I stopped in San Francisco on my return from Japan. Bruce met me at the airport, and we jumped into a chartered helicopter. It took us north from San Francisco, over Oakland, and out beyond majestic Mount Diablo. The land beneath us was barren but beautiful. It had rolling hills and long valleys, scattered ranches, walnut groves and desert brush.

I nodded at Bruce inside the helicopter. He was right. The property had potential. From the air, it was clear that development was moving in this direction. One subdivision had already been completed near the area; roads were being paved in other places in anticipation of future development.

"It's called Blackhawk Ranch," Bruce shouted above the noise of the rotors. "About 5,000 acres."

"I'm surprised it's available," I answered, looking down at a large round barn and well-maintained horse ranch.

"Named after a famous racehorse," Bruce shouted again. "I'm surprised it's available," I repeated.

"Only recently. Developers had it, but the operation went bankrupt. A dealer in heavy construction machinery bought it, built a home and just put the rest of the property back on the market."

As we continued to fly over the land, I imagined what it could look like: a couple of groomed golf courses, surrounded by homes, trees and retail property. We could develop a number of communities, similar to what we had done at the Woodlands in Florida. And there was potential for future expansion.

"It could be a medium- to high-end development," I said to Bruce. "We could probably put 5,000 single-family homes down there." I was enthusiastic but cautious.

"You like it?" Bruce asked.

"I want Bob to see this and hear what he thinks," I said. Bruce nodded. After flying over the property several more times, we returned to the airport.

Bob Carrau was a California homebuilder working for Leadership Housing, a division of Cerro. I liked him from the moment we had met during Cerro's purchase of my company. More important, I trusted his decisions, particularly since Leadership Housing had become successful in California and recently expanded into Florida. I contacted Bob and joined him to look at the site. He saw its possibilities as well.

"I'd take it all," he said.

I told him I wasn't interested in that, particularly because the owner had recently built a huge house on the property. He would sell it only if a buyer met his outrageous price. "I'm interested in maybe 4,000 acres," I said. "I see 4,000 acres with tremendous potential." Bob agreed. "I don't think you can lose," he said. Bob offered to help develop the land and the property if I made him a partner.

I was still living in Florida and had not considered moving to California. I would need someone of Bob's experience on the ground to see the project through, and his offer further confirmed our hopes. So did his willingness to leave Leadership and join me in the venture. Beyond this, I knew how difficult the California development process was. It included strong environmental protections. Bob's participation would be invaluable. I welcomed him as a partner and proceeded to buy the land. I acquired 4,000 acres for $4 million. I put down $400,000 and got the best 400 acres released for immediate development. I negotiated a 10-year note at 4 percent in 10 equal payments. Additional land would be released as I paid for it.

From my perspective, the arrangement was a no-lose deal. I soon realized just how important the terms would be to the success of the project. Though we had not discussed it in detail, Bob knew that developing Blackhawk would come with serious challenges, particularly from an environmental standpoint. The environmental law and approval process gave activists power against any major development. Their strategy was simple, and at the time was actually being taught as a formal course at the University of California, Berkeley. It was to intimidate county supervisors into limiting or rejecting a project and tie up development with lawsuits. Each suit forced a delay. After so many delays, developers could no longer afford to have their money tied up and unproductive. The cost of delays would become too high, and developers would either have to surrender, go bankrupt, or both.

Fortunately for us, the terms I structured with the seller did not tie up a lot of cash and allowed my team to fight back from a position of strength. That's what we did, as small threats from our opponents turned into what the media would come to call the Blackhawk Wars. Bob Carrau brought in a young hard-nosed attorney from Walnut Creek with remarkable attention to detail. His name was Dan VanVoorhis. He specialized in zoning and appeared to thrive in a hot political environment. The hotter the environment, the better he performed. He could out-analyze and out-talk anyone.

Our strategy was to ask for as much as possible from the very beginning—to start so big that after the other side pushed back, we'd still come out ahead. Our initial design was for a country club with two golf courses surrounded by 5,000 homes. It would be the biggest development ever planned for Northern California.

"You go that big and you're going to attract attention," someone warned. "I'd start out smaller."

"We're going to attract attention anyway," Dan said. "This way, if they cut us back, we still win."

They did try to cut. A group of local residents joined the Sierra Club and an organization named "Save Mount Diablo." They created a misleading picture of homes being constructed on the top of Mount Diablo. (We could not build there and did not want to. Much of the mountain was part of a state park.) The coalition circulated a petition and within 30 days collected 33,000 signatures against us—despite that fact that our development would be miles from the summit of the mountain and did not even interfere with Mount Diablo State Park. Their efforts were also energized by a broad-based campaign against the Walt Disney Company, which had proposed building a winter resort near Lake Tahoe. Every step we took would be met with a lawsuit, and the fight became so high-profile that the Sierra Club turned it into a fundraising opportunity.

Two activists led the fight against us. They were taking the Berkeley course and getting credit for their campaign. Their work was front-page news in the Contra Costa Times. Although both Dan and I refused to be intimidated, their stalling tactics were successful in delaying the project. After a few years, I believed the price of the property would never decrease and that I would eventually develop the land. So I purchased the site outright and put part of the land in trust for my children. Bob Carrau felt that he had taken the project as far as he could and was ready for a change.

I agreed that we needed a new team to move forward. During Christmas dinner in 1974, I approached Steve Beinke and Owen Schwaderer, members of my Florida organization. They thrived on hard work and were steadfast in their loyalty. Steve in his twenties and Owen in his early thirties, they were the youngest members of our group. They had distinguished themselves on a number of projects, including converting apartments to condominiums. With wives and children, they were eager to build a future with me in California. They would come to the state and join my former Florida attorney, Bill Morse.

As 1975 began, the new team went to work building positive relations with the county government. We understood the problems faced by our local officials, particularly having to deal with petitions opposing the project. We decided to address the situation in a practical way. Our strategy was to give the politicians victories that they could take back to their constituents. One of them was to gift 2,800 acres back to the government to enlarge Mount Diablo State Park and put a buffer between our development and the mountain. We would build on the remaining 1,200 acres that were best suited for homes. We also offered to cut the development to 2,500 homes, half of what we had proposed initially.

Five years after we had bought the land, our strategy finally paid off. By asking for everything, we received something, and that was enough to win approval of the project. Rather than build 5,000 high- and middle-income homes, we would build fewer. We'd make all the homes high-end so they'd sell only to wealthy professionals. So, in the end, we won, the environmentalists won and the county and state governments won. In fact, the only unfortunate part was that middle-class consumers could have benefited from our initial plan. We broke ground in June 1977.

Today, I believe the Blackhawk Wars succeeded in making the development one of the best in America. After we began building the high-end homes, I also won approval to build several middle-class communities in the area, particularly as we improved Crow Canyon Road leading into Blackhawk. While we were upgrading the road, I optioned some adjoining land at the unprecedented price of

$10,000 an acre and later got permission to build 5,000 units there. Chevron and Pacific Bell were moving employees into two large office buildings in the area. We built homes for their executives and apartments for their workers. The development, called Canyon Lakes, would eventually include 4,500 homes and a public golf course. It was completed in three years and made more money than Blackhawk. But our Blackhawk negotiations helped streamline the process. Later, I would build two developments on the other side of Mount Diablo, retirement communities similar to Tamarac.

Blackhawk would become my signature development and eventually my home. I constructed a 30,000-square-foot house there overlooking the country club. The idea of creating lifestyle-oriented communities became hugely popular in California, particularly for professionals in San Francisco and Oakland. They wanted more open space and larger homes in secluded and secure areas, and a sense of belonging.

The vision I had of the golf course and surrounding homes in the helicopter ride was finally becoming reality. Our team made certain the community was elegant in every detail. We controlled the architecture and color of every home built, as well as the landscaping and management of the two golf courses. A firm believer in advertising and public relations, I tied up the front page of the real estate sections of the *San Francisco Examiner* and the *San Francisco Chronicle* for an entire year. We dazzled residents and guests at the country club—one server wowed the crowds by pouring flaming dessert drinks! The marketing blitz created such a buzz that Blackhawk quickly sold out. The demand was so high that some of the lots that initially cost me $1,000 an acre are valued at more than $2 million today. This was a boon for my sons, who owned some of the property in trust. It made them all multimillionaires.

The fame of Blackhawk has spread around the world. Developers as far away as China named their own communities after ours and asked for my help in trying to duplicate its success. Eventually, I said yes. In Shanghai, I partnered with a local real estate company to create a high-end, world-class golf community, *The Sanctuary at Dongtan*. Located on Chongming Island, the location is known for its natural beauty including a wetlands and a bird preserve.

Most of the homes in Blackhawk have more than doubled in value. Even some people who fought us in the Blackhawk Wars have moved into the community. They now realize what can be done with land if it's developed properly. Along with moving tons of earth to build golf courses, lots for homes and beautiful water areas, we planted more than 400,000 trees. Today these trees have matured. They are beautiful.

It is a wonderful family community today. My own family loves it, including our 10 grandchildren. Pat and I have enjoyed spending more time with them in recent years. We have taken our kids and grandkids on trips to do humanitarian work (I discuss it more in coming chapters). We all celebrated my 80th birthday with a trip to China that included community service work.

Let me tell you about our grandkids for a moment. They have many talents and their own records of accomplishment in school and careers. Even though Pat and I never graduated from college, education is very important to us and we are very happy to see that all of our grandchildren will be college graduates and several will have advanced master's and doctoral degrees.

Jessica, Jeff's daughter, graduated from Cal Poly San Luis Obispo in Biology and worked in biological research. Her company sent her to the Boston University School of Medicine, where she is in a Ph.D. program in Molecular Medicine. She is doing biomedical/biochemical research in the vascular biology area. Colin is Jeff's second son and also attended Cal Poly San Luis Obispo, where he received a business degree. He worked in China for Morgan Stanley and then went to work for me in China real estate projects after attended an intensive Mandarin language program for seven months in Shanghai. He has lived in China most of the last seven years and is now fluent in Mandarin. John is Jeff's oldest son and is the only married grandchild (his wife's name is Melissa). He graduated from Cal Poly Pomona and does IT work for a company. Jeff's youngest son, Kyle, planned to attend the University of Colorado, Boulder, in 2013.

Renee is Mike's oldest daughter. She is currently working at Scholastic, Inc., as a Research Manager in Program Research and Validation. Renee holds an Ed.M. in Curriculum & Teaching, Early Childhood Education and a master's in Educational Psychology, Human Cognition & Learning—both from the Teachers College at Columbia University. Mike's first son, Brandon, was always very advanced in mathematics and science and completed his master's degree in math from New York University. He's been working as a math tutor for high school and college students, and he does SAT prep/test prep. Mike's next son, Patrick, is attending junior college and his youngest daughter, Elizabeth, has always been a superb student and will be graduating from high school in 2013.

David's daughter, Stephanie, graduates from high school as well in 2013. She has been very active in tennis, choir and pageants over the years. Christopher, his younger son, enters high school. He is an excellent student and tennis player and in two years plans on being an Eagle Scout, the first one in our family.

With Blackhawk, we were able to succeed because of the team we put together. Despite long periods of frustration and doubts, we never lost sight of what we wanted to create. I was clearly invested in the project. At one point, I owned all of the land. There was no way to develop it unless Blackhawk moved forward. The others were motivated by the battle and the possibilities of what Blackhawk could become. They were able to look beyond where we were at any given moment and stay focused on where we were going.

Blackhawk was going to be something special, and if the county government gave us the opportunity, we would prove it. Doug Dahlin was an invaluable member of our California group; he is one of the most gifted architects I know. He helped me bring to life what I had pictured during that helicopter ride. He captured my vision and improved it with his own talent in designing the community and styles of the homes, down to their interiors. That was key: to have each member of our team express his respective genius in the details. Good thing for me—I am not a detail person. I don't have the patience to get down into the weeds. The dynamic of Steve, Owen, Dan and Doug balanced perfectly with my vision. We were able to inspire and motivate one another, even during the darkest days of the Blackhawk Wars.

Later, I asked Steve Beinke what he believed was the most important lesson we learned from the Blackhawk Wars. Without hesitation, he answered, the need to be sincerely involved in the community, to immerse ourselves so people come to know and trust us. We began winning the Blackhawk Wars when we began listening to the concerns of others and letting them know that we understood how they felt and were willing to address their needs. We began winning when we looked at the situation from the point of view of the local community and of county leaders who had to make decisions to satisfy all constituencies.

"Nothing is more important than working directly with the people," Steve said. "You can't simply hire consultants, make a plan and say, 'This is it.' That won't work anymore, especially in sensitive areas like California, Florida and the Northwest. Large projects cannot proceed in these areas anymore without the developers being a part of the community, trusted and known to put the interests of the community ahead of their own."

Steve is right. Blackhawk taught us—as I have learned many other times through the years—that there is no substitute for credibility and goodwill, important assets for leadership. In any endeavor they provide the foundation for success.

Part III

Different

Chapter 6:
FROM BLACKHAWK TO THE SEAHAWKS

When one door closes, another opens.

Alexander Graham Bell

In 1988, I did something that many American boys dream about: I bought a professional football team, the Seattle Seahawks. That was different, for certain. The team was an expansion organization that had seen its share of ups and downs in its few years of existence.

The Nordstrom family owned it. The Nordstroms were good friends, particularly the late Jim Nordstrom, one of the most honorable businessmen I've ever known. And Seattle is a wonderful city. There are many diehard Seahawks fans. A large and active press corps followed the sport. But the team had yet to catch fire the way other franchises had, especially in larger markets. I felt we could do a lot to build the program. I was up to the challenge. Most important, the purchase worked on a business level.

Jim Nordstrom was one of the best salesmen in the world— just look at the success of his family's chain of department stores.

I thought I'd learned something about the art after 30 years in sales myself. But Jim Nordstrom took me back to school. He had invited me to Washington to discuss business unrelated to football. Unknown to me, his family had decided to sell the Seahawks. Some members wanted to get out of football to concentrate on retailing. It was no coincidence, then, that on the way back to the airport for my return flight to Northern California, Jim asked if I wouldn't mind making a detour.

We ended up at the Seahawks' practice field. Within a few minutes, all my memories of high school football came rushing back. Jim introduced me to players who were quickly becoming legends—stars like Steve Largent and Brian Bosworth—and the coaches under the leadership of Chuck Knox. The experience was larger than life. I guess enthusiasm showed in my eyes. Jim didn't waste any time; he said he was looking for a buyer for the team. We briefly discussed price, and by the time I arrived at the airport to catch my flight, we had shaken hands.

I paid $79 million for the Seahawks. I owned a majority of the team. My friend Ken Hofmann, a California developer who was one of the owners of the Oakland A's baseball franchise, came in for 25 percent. Steve Beinke of my company bought 6 percent and a few other close friends purchased 1 percent each. Part of my motivation—and the reason I was able to make a quick decision—was that the purchase worked for me on a tax level. It provided me with an opportunity to take some of my ordinary income, taxed at higher rates, and shelter it with the depreciation charges of player salaries. But I couldn't hide my excitement when I spoke with my son David after I returned to California. I knew that if anyone could share how I felt, it would be David. He had not only been a standout player in high school but was one of the most devoted fans of professional football I knew.

After the Nordstroms announced the sale, I went to Seattle for a press conference. There was a lot of publicity, both in the newspapers and on TV. I became an instant celebrity. Suddenly, I was famous. When I walked down the street, everyone would point or look at me. It was much different from being a builder. Whenever there was a game, fans would stop me on the way into the stadium. Eventually, I needed a police escort to get up to the owner's box at the stadium, which was called the Kingdome. I grew to enjoy it. My box seated 40 guests. I loved asking friends and celebrities to join me. We always had good food and the best seats in the house. I enjoyed football so much that I started standing on the sidelines with the players. You could feel the intensity of the game. If you won, the locker room afterward was the highlight of the night. If you lost, you immediately went home. There was a famous bar and restaurant near the stadium, McCrory's, where everyone went when the game ended. After victories, it was crowded and I was the celebrity of the moment.

Owning the Seahawks actually delighted the entire family. Two of my sons, David and Scott, became involved in the organization, and we attended the games as a group. We often flew to Seattle on a DC-9 I had purchased as a corporate jet. The fans welcomed us, and it appeared that the future was bright. We finished my first season as owner with a 9-7 record, the best ever for the Seahawks. We had won the challenging AFC West division and lost a first-round playoff game to Cincinnati in a heartbreaker. The Seahawks had never won a division title before.

For a while, it appeared that the sky was the limit. It was a pleasure to work with the local community and speak to business and civic organizations. The fans were optimistic about the future. I enjoyed being around them and being part of the energy of the National Football League, an exclusive club. The owners included many of the household names that had built the league. They were great men from great families. They were motivated more by their desire to make professional football the most popular sport in the world than by personal greed. It was as much a mission as it was a profession. To be around them—and to be associated with the greatest athletes in the world—seemed like a dream.

I enjoyed Seattle and decided to move there. We bought a home on an island, near the Nordstrom family. I also purchased a condominium close to the team offices and spent as much time as I could there and with fans. I had learned a hard lesson from jumping into Modiflex Homes before I fully understood the industry, so I was determined to keep the decision-making for the team with the people who had the expertise. That meant the general manager, the coaches and the scouts. I took a deliberate hands-off approach. I limited my involvement to sitting with my family and friends in the owner's box of the Kingdome and attending the owners' meetings.

But after we finished the following season at 8-8, I felt my management style needed some changes. From my perspective, there were several problems. Many of our draft selections did not pan out. Our conditioning program had room for improvement. And our team was not making enough revenue to land top talent. I watched, frustrated, as top players went to teams in larger markets with more lucrative stadium deals. We had some of the finest linemen in the league, but we lacked a quarterback who could make things happen. And our running backs were not strong enough to balance our offensive attack.

For a while, the team appeared one-dimensional, relying heavily on Steve Largent, our star receiver, to carry the team. That was not going to get us where we wanted to be—a divisional powerhouse with a playoff victory or two en route to an eventual Super Bowl.

Tom Flores, a top coach, had been a friend for some time. He had proven himself a winner with the 1981 World Champion Oakland Raiders and the 1984 World Champion L.A. Raiders. I offered him total freedom if he would come in as general manager and work with

Chuck Knox to build us a top team. He agreed and took over operations. Again, I stepped back and waited for his assessment. It came loud and clear after the 1990 season, which ended with a disappointing 7-8. Tom felt that if he was going to be responsible for turning the team around, he also needed to take over as head coach. We discussed the idea seriously. I liked Chuck Knox. He was a player's coach, with one of the best records in the league. But I could not honestly say that he was getting everything he needed to produce the kind of winning team I wanted.

A long-term lease between the Seahawks and King County, owner of the Kingdome, was hurting our ability to develop the franchise. The economics weren't working. Teams shared television revenue equally and split ticket sales revenue 60/40 (60 percent for the home team, 40 percent for the visiting team). But stronger teams had stadium agreements that also let them raise working capital through concession sales, skyboxes, club seating, parking and advertising.

We had almost none of that in the Kingdome. The stadium was small, with only a few skyboxes shared between us; the baseball team, the Mariners, and the Kingdome. When we asked the county to renegotiate our lease, it wouldn't budge. So I didn't have many alternatives. I believed Chuck was doing the best he could with what he had, but I also needed to give Tom the authority to do what was necessary to create a winning team. With that, I removed Chuck and made Tom general manager, president and head coach. He took charge of our recruiting, and we signed a few players who gave us reason to hope.

Unfortunately, our conditioning program was still weak. Our players were not in top shape. As in the previous two seasons, we lost a handful of games in the final minutes and by only a few points—a sure sign of conditioning troubles. But things went from bad to worse. That season, 26 of our players, including six linebackers, were out with injuries. The situation had deteriorated so much that by the end of the season, we were literally hiring players only days before a game. The consequences were devastating. We ended the season 2-14. The press ripped into me. Many of the attacks were personal; I was referred to as a "Bubba" or "Bozo," and the "wealthy California developer" tag, never popular in Seattle, caused more resentment than ever. I tried not to think about them, but they troubled me, particularly because they upset my family.

From the day I bought the team, my son David had been an asset to me. He had studied the team and game closely. From the beginning, he was unofficially involved in the decision-making. He had studied the scouting reports and participated in the drafts. He had learned the front office and taken the time to reach out to the community. He also had attended the owners' meetings with me and built friendships with sons of other owners who were stepping into important roles within the league. I talked to Tom about stepping aside as president and putting David in that position. I told Tom I was concerned that having one man wear three vital hats diluted his focus and ability to function at his best. Most NFL teams have had similar experiences when the head coach was given this much responsibility.

It was not an easy discussion. Tom realized that a head coach who serves as president is often conflicted and unable to work properly with his athletes. For example, a coach who is trying to persuade a recruit to play for him while at the same time negotiating that player's salary is in a tough position. So is a coach who is forced to worry about gate receipts, community outreach and promotional events.

We all realized what needed to be done, and in December 1992, I named David president of the Seahawks organization. I was proud of him and the way he worked. He kept the front office intact and developed a healthy relationship with Tom. His first priority was to sit down with the team physicians and determine what had happened to our players. Twenty-six injuries was not normal or acceptable.

Clearly, we needed to change our conditioning program. David made those changes. He also went to work with the media and fans to repair relationships that had been deteriorating. He worked with other NFL owners to understand the coming changes in the league, including the salary cap, which was initiated in his first year.

That year, the team came back with a 6-10 record. Again, it could have been better, but some factors were out of our control. For example, David successfully acquired two prime free agents—offensive lineman Howard "House" Ballard and two-time All Pro cornerback Nate Odomes. Signing them was considered a coup and upgrading these two positions was critical to our future. Tom and David built a strategy and offered each player $8 million over four years. For a short time, it appeared the media were behind us again. Fans were excited. Expectations for the '94 season were high. I believed we would surpass the .500 mark and even win the division.

Then we got the call. Just weeks before training camp, Nate Odomes injured his knee in a basketball game. He had torn a ligament, required an operation and was lost for the season. It was a big blow to the organization, as was Nate's insistence that his orthopedic surgeon perform the operation. Despite our investment, we would have no control over the outcome. That outcome would prove even more troubling when he returned for the '95 season, only to tear the same ligament the second week of practice. This time, he allowed our doctor to operate. He sat out his second consecutive season and came back the third year, but failed to make the team. We finished the '94 season at 6-10, no improvement on the previous year.

We also knew we needed a quarterback. Two previous first round selections, Kelly Stouffer and Dan McGuire, failed to develop and eventually were released. Then in 1993, we believed our search was over. We signed Rick Mirer out of Notre Dame. He was supposed to be in the mold of Joe Montana and, along with Drew Bledsoe, was one of the top picks in that draft. Although we preferred Bledsoe, our scouts placed Rick just behind him on the draft board. We missed Drew by a hair.

Rick had a good rookie season. He showed a strong arm and leadership ability. Rick could also scramble. We believed this was what we needed to make things happen on the field. His challenge was being able (or unable) to read defense. His tendency was to focus on only his first or second receiver, allowing cornerbacks to play off his eyes. His interceptions climbed and his touchdown and passing statistics declined at a steady rate.

Even with a new quarterback, we didn't improve our record. I realized the time had come to make a change at the head coach position. It was a decision that would prove to be as difficult as anything I'd done professionally. Tom was a long-time friend. I had talked him into coming to Seattle. He had the respect of the players and was a proven winner. But it was not working with the Seahawks.

Our conversation wasn't long. He realized a change was necessary—anything to find the chemistry needed to win. We brought in Dennis Erickson, a college coach who had won two national championships at the University of Miami. Despite his appointment, we still did not improve the next season. We still had a problem at quarterback and we were playing in probably the toughest division in the NFL, the AFC West. During the first half of the 1990s, it seemed like the Chiefs, Chargers and Broncos were always in the playoff picture.

Things got worse. Under the new 1993 collective bargaining agreement with players, several teams began offering huge signing bonuses to them. They'd be paid over several years. With this development, I realized we wouldn't be able to compete for players without some big changes. To bring in needed revenue, we'd need a new lease or a new stadium. Among other things, we had to divide our skybox income and advertising with the Mariners. We tried again to negotiate with the county about our concerns. We wanted money for stadium improvements. The Mariners and Seahawks jointly pursued stadium funding from the state legislature. The legislature declined, and it became obvious that it was going to be almost impossible for us to get a new stadium or improvements to keep us competitive.

I made the difficult decision to either move the team or find a buyer in Seattle who would have a better chance of getting a new stadium. I approached potential buyers in Los Angeles and Anaheim. At the same time, we contacted prospects in Seattle. No one was interested, especially after they investigated our stadium lease.

Finally, I felt I had no other choice. We moved our preseason practice to Anaheim and announced that we would find another home for the team. Seattle erupted in anger. We got hit with many lawsuits to stop us from moving. But the city also got serious about helping us find a buyer. Local leaders finally persuaded Paul Allen, a Seattle resident and the cofounder of Microsoft, to option the team for $200 million. But the state and county had to build him a new stadium.

Allen put down $30 million as a deposit. I'd have to return his money if he failed to get his stadium. He spent millions of dollars on a campaign to persuade voters to approve a new facility. While we had originally requested only $120 million to modernize the King-dome, the government would now be contributing $300 million to build the new stadium. The referendum barely passed. We closed the sale at the end of 1997.

Once again I was starting over—without football, but with the money and time to look for real purpose in my life.

Chapter 7:
LEADING ME TO PURPOSE

Before you are a leader,
success is all about growing yourself.
When you become a leader,
success is all about growing others.

Jack Welch

I have been in the car business, the real estate business and the sports business.

Now I want to be the leadership business.

My journey to this purpose has had many twists and turns, as the pages that follow will show. Only recently have I seen the pieces of a plan to help develop the world's future leaders come together. It's through several charitable ventures I launched that at first appeared different and disconnected. Now the connections are clear.

If I have learned one thing in nearly seven decades in business and more than a decade of philanthropy, it is that the world needs leaders. It faces serious social, economic and political challenges in the years ahead, from shrinking global resources and increasing reliance on entitlements and damage to the environment, to international conflict and the threat of terrorism and nuclear war. We will need strong, smart, dedicated leaders—a lot of them—to tackle these problems and others.

I believe everyone is born with leadership skills and qualities. Within a family, one member may emerge as the leader because of age and experience—a matriarch or patriarch. Or during a family crisis, one sibling may rise above the others to take charge. Leaders in sport teams are usually apparent because of their superior athletic ability, knowledge of the game, intelligence, longevity or hard work. In places of worship, parishioners will elect members to leadership positions to manage a congregation's operations and finances. In a community, certain homeowners will lead neighborhood watch groups to guard against crime. In schools, students will pick peers to head their many clubs and activities. It is natural for humans to select leaders in society, to help create order, provide guidance and accomplish goals—the same as it is in nature in the animal world.

Taking charge in a smaller group is not diminished by its size— we need leaders in every organization, small and large, and are grateful to all who serve in leadership roles. But my interest is in exceptional, highly skilled leadership at the highest levels—in business, government, education, science, medicine, the arts and other disciplines. I want to help develop leaders who will take on the world's big problems and challenges and fix them with strong, creative ideas and solutions. I know they are out there, though they themselves may not know it yet. I believe now that finding and developing them is my purpose. I've learned that with time.

Take Nina D'Amato, for instance. As a major in the U.S. Marine Corps, she put her life on the line every day in one of the most dangerous places in the world, Helmand Province in Afghanistan. Her orders were to help the Afghan government rebuild and sustain schools. In other parts of Afghanistan, that job had been handled by nongovernmental and aid organizations. But not in Helmand, which remained a Taliban stronghold. The Taliban had specifically targeted

The elderly man in Romania who had suffered a stroke and whose plight moved me to start the Wheelchair Foundation.

The elderly Vietnamese woman who told me she had wanted to die—until she got a new wheelchair.

The Guatemalan man with gangrene who did not want $25 from me for anesthesia for his leg amputation. We insisted he take it.

Pat and I in South Africa in 2001 distributing wheelchairs with Nelson Mandela.

The president of Namibia, Sam Nujoma, reads his remarks at our distribution there in 2001.

Dr. Robert A. Schuller from Crystal Cathedral Ministries with his wife, Donna, at our distribution on the bridge at Victoria Falls in Africa in 2003.

Meeting the first lady of Tanzania, Anna Mkapa, who is a member of our International Board of Advisors.

One of our distributions in South Africa with our friends from SPAR stores.

Meeting with the first lady of Nigeria, Stella Obasanjo, at a distribution in her country in 2001.

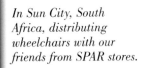

In Sun City, South Africa, distributing wheelchairs with our friends from SPAR stores.

Pat and I met a man who crawled to get to our wheelchair distribution in Zimbabwe.

Some of these African women are land mine victims and are in need of wheelchairs.

A man coming to our distribution in Afghanistan in 2003. Most people in his condition are land mine victims.

Wheelchairs can change lives immediately. One minute, this boy in Laos who lost his leg to a land mine is standing with crutches; the next minute, he is mobile in a new wheelchair.

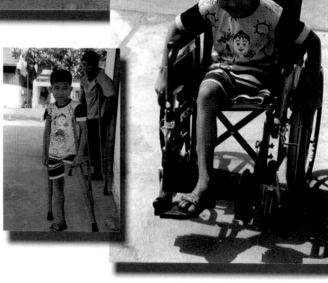

With my good friend King Juan Carlos of Spain (left), and his wife, Queen Sofia, and the president and first lady of Brazil in 2000. The king and queen chair our International Board of Advisors.

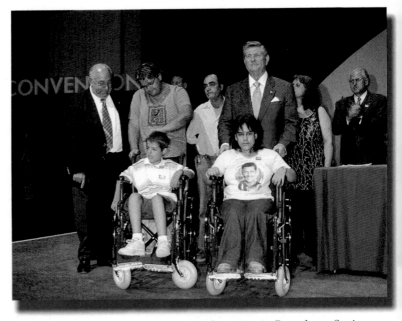

Joining Rotarians at their international meeting in Barcelona, Spain, in 2002. Rick King, the organization's president, is in the center front. Dr. Jon Grant is in the back on the right.

I traveled to Saudi Arabia in 2004 to work on an agreement to distribute wheelchairs in this vital region of the world.

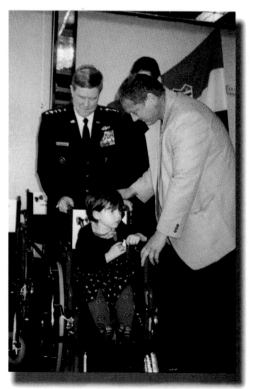

General Joe Ralston (USAF-Ret.) helps at a wheelchair distribution in Eastern Europe. He is a member of our International Board of Advisors.

Meeting with First Lady Ruby Moscoso de Young and her sister, President Mireya Elisa Moscoso Rodriguez, at a distribution in Panama in 2001.

Distributing wheelchairs in Guatemala with Evelyn de Portillo, when she was first lady of that country.

Pat and I with our friend, Frank Devlyn, the former president of the Rotarians who first got them involved with the Wheelchair Foundation. With us are his wife, Gloria Rita, and the first lady of Mexico, Martha Sahagun Fox (center), who is a member of our International Board of Advisors.

A nun we helped in Honduras in 2001.

Distributing wheelchairs with friends from the LDS Church.

With Angel, the boy in Mexico who said he would "see me in heaven."

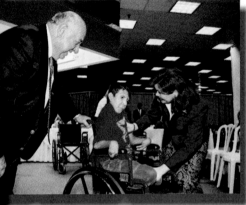

Jacalyn Leavitt, the former first lady of Utah, meets a wheelchair recipient with me in Puerto Rico.

I greet a wheelchair recipient at a distribution in El Salvador.

Jon and Linda Grant, two of our most committed Rotary fundraisers and volunteers, on a wheelchair distribution in Africa.

My son David, president of the Wheelchair Foundation, with his classmates from Princeton University and family members at a distribution in Peru in 2012.

Vietnam veterans and their spouses returned to Vietnam in 2012 to distribute wheelchairs on a mission of peace and healing.

With a wheelchair recipient at our distribution in Afghanistan in 2003.

With Bui Thi Huyen, the Vietnamese girl I met in 2000, whose joy at receiving a wheelchair helped convince me to start the Wheelchair Foundation.

*His All Holiness Ecumenical Patriarch Bartholomew in 2004
at a distribution with me in Turkey.*

*Receiving a blessing from His Holiness Pope John Paul II in 2004, with my
Wheelchair Foundation colleague Charli Butterfield.*

A Chinese man helps a family member into one of our wheelchairs at a distribution in China.

Deng Pufang, founder of the China Disabled Persons' Federation, and me in 2001. He is a member of our International Board of Advisors.

A kiss for a wonderful young lady in China, 2004.

I am honored to meet wheelchair recipient Xie Yanhong of China, the first physically disabled man to swim the English Channel.

Meeting more wheelchair recipients in China, 2004. I give each one a handshake and a smile.

Kun Sha, a Chinese orphan, sang to me when he received his wheelchair from us in 2002.

Kun Sha today, all grown up and a flourishing student.

Employees of IBM China distributed wheelchairs to physically disabled people in Shanghai in 2012.

Employees of Qualcomm in Shanghai did a distribution, too.

schools there for attack—burning them down in some instances—to try to prevent the government from reestablishing authority and civil order and to continue to terrorize citizens—common thugs just trying to intimidate and hold on to power following the U.S. invasion of Afghanistan in the wake of 9/11.

After U.S. troops surged into the province in 2010 to defeat the last Taliban combatants and establish security, the Marines and Afghan leaders began restoring the education system there, renovating school buildings and setting up temporary "tent schools" to get kids back to class—especially girls, who had been forbidden by the Taliban to receive a formal education. Under Major D'Amato's leadership, authorities opened and operated 115 brick-and-mortar schools, and 30 tent schools, for 85,000 children in Helmand Province. A quarter of them were girls.

"Communities will not plan for education unless it's safe and secure," Major D'Amato told the San Francisco Chronicle in 2011. "Schools evoke a lot of hope in people."

I agree. That's why I helped start the Behring Principal Leadership Institute in 2000 at the University of California, Berkeley.

Major D'Amato attended it.

In 2007, Nina D'Amato worked at A.P. Giannini Middle School in San Francisco. She had first joined in the Marine Corps right out of college. But when her duty ended, she pursued her passion to become a teacher. She loved her job, but came to feel that public schools could be better and that the only way to truly change them was to become a leader. She enrolled in the Principal Leadership Institute, which I helped launch as part of a $7.5 million gift to Berkeley. It prepares educators to be effective leaders in California's urban schools, where reform and improvement is most needed but most difficult. The majority of the students accepted into the Institute are teachers from inner-city schools. The funds I donated provided scholarships of up to $10,000 to help cover the cost of tuition for each student. After an intensive 15-month program of night, weekend and summer school courses, students receive a master's degree in education with a state administrative certification to enter into leadership positions. Graduates agree to serve in a leadership capacity in a California public school for four years. Major D'Amato graduated in 2008.

"The Principal Leadership Institute at UC Berkeley sponsored by Kenneth E. Behring was not only rigorous, but firmly anchored the truth that data and feedback loops are central to success," she said. "Frameworks are how senior leaders ingest information in complex environments, and it is incumbent upon all leaders in an organization to articulate and communicate visions and missions to all stakeholders. Equally important is to ensure you are ready and able to defend the strategy. I'm thankful for the opportunity to have been pressed in a safe place like UC Berkeley, because in Afghanistan, the stakes became much, much higher."

Major D'Amato was awarded a Meritorious Service Medal for her work in Afghanistan and was recently selected by the University of California Alumni Association for the 2013 Mark Bingham Award for Excellence in Achievement by a Young Alumna for her commitment to education. I'm pleased and humbled that my support for the Institute helped Major D'Amato develop her leadership skills, which in turn helped her in her mission in Afghanistan and, through her success, helped thousands of Afghan families find hope, opportunity and peace.

Back in 2000, I had no idea that the Behring Principal Leadership Institute might end up assisting struggling people in a war-torn country on the other side of the world or that it could have such a big impact. I was trying to fix schools in California. I did not know a lot of things about philanthropy back then; it was something new to me. I'd achieved more financial success than most people dream of. I'd made hundreds of millions of dollars and owned a professional football team. I fly around the world in my own private jet. I liked that lifestyle. I still like it. But you get to the point in life where you look at yourself, look at the world and realize it's been extremely good to you and it's time to give something back.

That made me feel good, whether in my heart, with the private joy helping others brings, or to my heart, with the recognition and satisfaction it brings. So I wanted to do more of it—and in a big way, like I have lived and done everything in my life. I decided I wanted to help as many people as possible—millions of them—in the time I had left on this Earth. But equally important, I wanted to share and teach the experience of giving to millions, too, even if they themselves might have the time, talent or treasure to help just one person.

"Whoever saves one life saves the world entire," the Talmud teaches. That is no small thing. It adds up.

And learning to give back is critical step in becoming a leader.

In Shanghai, China, 3,000 miles from Helmand Province, Hainan Yin has learned about the joy of giving, which has helped him become a leader. In 2012, Hainan was a warranty manager for a division of IBM China. When IBM hired Hainan, it said part of his job involved organizing corporate teambuilding. Hainan believed one way to accomplish this was to get his company and co-workers to support physically disabled people in Shanghai.

He partnered with the manager of a local community center and Wheelchair Foundation. After meeting many physically disabled people in my travels around the world, I started the foundation in 2000 with an initial pledge of $15 million. It gives away free wheelchairs to tens of thousands of people with physical disabilities each year. With additional financial support from caring individuals, companies and nonprofit organizations, the foundation is now on track to deliver its one-millionth wheelchair.

Together, Hainan and the Wheelchair Foundation's China

division organized a picnic for disabled people at a local park as part of the foundation's "Redchair Project" in Shanghai (all of our wheelchairs are red). IBM employees donated the funding to give away 20 wheelchairs at the event and workers volunteered their time to staff it. According to Hainan, the IBM employees said it was the "most rewarding teambuilding exercise" they'd ever done. Not only were they able to get to know one another better, they were able to give the gift of mobility to those who had never had it. The picnic was such a success that Hainan launched the IBM Shanghai Volunteer Association and created a formal partnership with the foundation.

"When you help others you are very happy and just you have a lot of sense of achievement," Hainan says.

Gretchen Mohr is becoming a leader thanks to another nonprofit venture I support, National History Day. NHD seeks to bring history to life for middle school and high school students though in-depth, extracurricular research projects. Students present their findings in local, state and national competitions with papers, exhibits, documentaries, performances and websites. This requires strong research and organizational skills—capabilities leaders need.

Gretchen, a high school senior from Long Grove, Iowa, began participating in NHD in seventh grade, entering the documentary category every time. In ninth grade, her film was about Dr. Norman Borlaug, the Nobel Prize-winning agronomist whose research in plant breeding and genetics helped increase global food productivity and fight hunger. Inspired, Gretchen founded and organized the first Dr. Borlaug Quad Cities Youth Hunger Summit in 2012 in surrounding communities in Iowa and Illinois. About 250 students from 16 high schools in the area participated, hearing from 32 experts in the field. The kids packaged more 26,200 meals for families in their community.

"I hope that by doing this, I have helped motivate my generation to become some of Dr. Borlaug's 'hunger fighters,' " Gretchen said.

"NHD motives students to go above and beyond. The organizational skills I acquired from my NHD work served me well in planning the symposium." Gretchen told a local TV news reporter: "High school students are the next generation. If we want to see an end to world hunger in our lifetime, it's going to be the kids that are going to do it."

Exactly right.

Helen Hong is taking the lead in saving endangered birds in Beijing, China. Helen, an eighth-grader at the Beijing International School, was a participant in an education program I modeled after NHD, Global Natural History Day, which launched in China in 2012. I believe the natural sciences, particularly the animal world, offer important lessons to mankind. GNHD engages kids in research projects to help them learn them.

Helen chose a bird called the Beijing swift for her project in 2012; it is threatened with extinction because of urban develop-ment. She heard about the swift from her parents, who told her that when they were kids, they'd see swarms of swallows flying across the sky. For her project, Helen was determined to track down sur-viving swallows. In her free time on weekends, Helen traveled around Beijing looking for the birds and their habitat. Helen con-ducted a one-on-one interview with one of the top researchers on the Beijing swift at China's Institute of Zoology. After completing her project and the competition—she won first prize in the international division—Helen established her own nonprofit organization, the Swift Action Foundation, to raise awareness of the bird's plight.

"I want to bring awareness to this species, which was once a big part of people's lives but is now slowly fading away," Helen wrote in her exhibit proposal. "I also want to help people to pay more atten-tion to species that aren't yet endangered and help to protect them before it's too late."

Dev Thakar wants to be a leader too. Dev, a fourth-grade student from Fremont, California, plans to be president of the United States when he grows up. If he does, he will likely make history for being the first president born in the U.S. to immigrants from India.

Dev and his family were in Washington, DC, in 2012 to visit the Smithsonian Institution's National Museum of American History. His parents, Jig and Sejal, who immigrated to the U.S. from India in 1998, wanted him and his older sister, Devanshi, to learn about the history of the U.S., especially the opportunities it offers its citizens and the sacrifices generations of Americans made to protect them. The family had just come from an exhibition called "The American Presidency: A Glorious Burden." Dev stood proudly at a replica of a presidential podium, complete with the Seal of the President of the United States, to have his picture taken by his parents.

Dev not only learned a lot about the U.S. and its leaders at the Smithsonian, he was also inspired to become a leader. "I want to help other citizens. I want to help the nation," Dev says of his ambitions for the White House.

Me, too—which is why I have financially supported the Smithsonian. I first donated to its Museum of Natural History and then to its the American History Museum. In total, I committed $100 million over 10 years. That's because I believe more than ever that museums can be more than fun places to visit with your family on a weekend afternoon—they can be powerful teaching tools, cathedrals of learning and schools for leaders. In fact, I believe in the role of museums in education so strongly now that I am doubling down on my support for them, starting with a dozen museums in China.

This is just the beginning. The Behring Principal Leadership Institute, the Wheelchair Foundation, the National Museum of American History, Global Natural History Day, National History Day and my other philanthropic activities have all proven to me the tremendous possibility and potential of helping to create generations of future leaders. I have big plans and big dreams for this goal and believe all of these seemingly different endeavors can support one great leadership development program under my new charitable organization, the Global Health and Education Foundation. After you read more of our stories about giving and receiving gifts of learning, good health, mobility, independence and self-reliance, I hope you will get excited, too, and join me to make this dream a reality! We are off to a promising start, with leaders like Nina D'Amato, Gretchen Mohr, and Helen Hong already making the world a better place.

But in my excitement to tell you all about it, I have gotten ahead of myself. So come back with me now to where it all began, to a village in Romania many years ago...

Part IV

Purpose

Chapter 8:
EPIPHANIES

Life without hope
is life without meaning.

Anonymous

There are some experiences that change you forever. They leave you with a different impression of the world and the people in it, and you are forced to act on this new understanding. At least I've been forced to act on it. Robert Berdahl, chancellor of the University of California, Berkeley, once described me as "a man who sees a need and responds immediately." From my earliest days as a used car salesman turned snowplow operator, I've always reacted quickly to any situation involving a need waiting to be filled.

In a remote village in Romania in 1999, a handful of people exposed me to a world that I never knew existed. Their simple wish to enjoy freedom of mobility moved me to take action. Meeting them and thousands of people in the world like them changed the course of my life. It brought me true joy. It helped me to find real purpose.

This journey began in Africa. In the 1990s, I was making

frequent hunting trips to Zambia, Zimbabwe and Namibia. Our hunting parties included local trackers and professional hunters. They'd take me to villages to visit schools and health clinics. Though I'd grown up poor in rural Wisconsin, nothing prepared me for what I saw. The hospitals were sometimes single large rooms partitioned off so that women in labor were barely separated from children with malaria or people waiting for surgery. The beds were small and sometimes not even covered with sheets. The facilities were so overcrowded that sometimes people had to lie on the floor. Doctors and nurses didn't have adequate medical supplies or equipment. I was shocked by the conditions.

Schools also lacked basic necessities. Usually they were nothing more than a simple shelter without doors or windows. In some places, they consisted of a few sheets hung from tree branches. Kids came to class barefoot; there were no books or supplies for them. Teachers had difficulty teaching them reading and writing, let alone anything beyond basic skills, because of the lack of educational materials. So by the second or third grade, many children lost interest in learning. I met devoted teachers who were discouraged because they had difficulty keeping the children in class. They felt that because their students couldn't get a decent education, they would simply return to the same impoverished village life of their parents and would be unable to improve themselves or their communities. Their comments struck me.

When I returned home from Africa, I started looking for medical and school supplies to bring back with me on my next trip. Because there are so many different languages and dialects within single countries in Africa, their governments encourage people to learn English. In many places, it's become the unifying language and the language of business. One of the best tools for teaching people English is children's books, which are written simply. I contacted some school districts in California that were replacing some of their older texts for first-, second- and third-graders. They agreed to donate these old books to African schools. My friends in the Bich family of France even agreed to donate 100,000 Bic pens. I gathered these and other supplies and packed them into my plane to take to Africa. On my next trip, my team and I made sure the items were distributed in needy villages.

Each time I returned to Africa, I brought a load of medical supplies, school supplies or clothes to the villages near the places I was visiting. Eventually, the shipments got so big that I arranged for some of them to be sent in separate containers. I felt the materials were making a difference in the communities that received them.

Charitable organizations in the U.S. heard about what I was doing and started to call me with requests. In 1999, LDS Charities asked if I could deliver supplies near the route we were taking to Africa. LDS Charities is the humanitarian outreach branch of The Church of Jesus Christ of Latter-day Saints. It provides assistance to people in need, regardless of race or religion worldwide. When families were forced to flee Kosovo in the 1990s, LDS Charities responded immediately with food, clothing, blankets and personal hygiene kits. The organization wanted to deliver 15 tons of canned meat quickly to the refugees there and asked for my help. I agreed. When we loaded the plane, we had room left in the hold. Some of the volunteers asked if I wouldn't mind stopping in Romania to deliver wheelchairs to a hospital there. We had space for six wheelchairs. Little did I know that these six wheelchairs would change the direction of my life.

After delivering the meat to the refugee camps, I flew to Romania. The hospital we went to wasn't as bad as those I had visited in Africa, but it was not in good shape. In the U.S., we take for granted that our hospitals will be clean and sanitary and have all of the medical supplies we might need. That's not the case in much of the world. I met the hospital director when we dropped off the wheelchairs. He showed me around the facility and talked to me about the lives of people with disabilities. He said that in poor and developing countries, many people with physical disabilities are basically discarded. They often aren't treated as human beings. As a result of their illnesses or inability to move, they and their families are stigmatized. There's a belief in some cultures that if a child is born with a physical disability, it is punishment for something that the families have done wrong. In parts of the world, the disabled are treated as if they are cursed or possessed by evil spirits. Neighbors don't acknowledge their presence. They can be hidden away in the back of a hut and given a single daily meal. Sometimes their families are ashamed to see them crawl or be carried, so they lock them away. I have seen people kept in boxes in back rooms.

The director introduced me to an elderly man who had lost his wife and then suffered a stroke. He couldn't walk anymore. The man couldn't speak any English, but the hospital staff interpreted his story for me. I told him that I had brought a wheelchair for him so that he would be able to move on his own again. When I helped lift him into the wheelchair, he started to cry. Through his tears, he explained that now he would be free to leave his house when he went home.

"Now I can go outside in my yard and smoke with my neighbors," he said.

All I could say to him was, "I'm happy we could help you."

I was deeply moved. I found it unbelievable that this man and others like him were denied the smallest pleasures in life because of their disabilities. I'd never spent any time with immobile people. The simple gift of a wheelchair literally transformed this man's life. It meant so much to him.

I have never felt as grateful as I did in that moment. It took so little to give a wheelchair, but yet it meant so much. I was amazed—I had helped give someone the gift of mobility and independence—a gift of a new life. I realized that I'd found something tangible and worthwhile, something that sparked an interest within me.

When I returned home from Romania, I thought about what had happened. I had previously seen wheelchairs as a form of confinement. I didn't comprehend the liberation that one could bring to those who are unable to afford them. I was intrigued by the difference these wheelchairs could make in a person's life and I wanted to find other ways to reach out.

I made contact with a charitable organization in Iowa, Hope Haven Ministries, which refurbished wheelchairs and had already planned a delivery to Vietnam in March 2000. It just needed someone to sponsor the shipment. I agreed, as I long as I could join the delivery. In late March, I flew to Vietnam and met the group. As we waited for the wheelchairs to clear customs, we were invited to a hospital. The conditions were unimaginable. Sick people were stacked in every room. The facility did not have enough nurses and help to adequately care for patients. The bathrooms and halls were unsanitary. We went into one room that housed three men with leprosy. They were badly disfigured; they had swollen lumps on their hands and feet and growing out of their heads. I hesitated at first, but I felt compelled to talk to them. When I reached out to touch them, they smiled and tears filled their eyes. Someone had finally shown them friendship and kindness.

With the help of a doctor at the hospital, we convinced the government to release some of the wheelchairs to us later that day. One of our first deliveries was to a young girl in a small village outside of Hanoi. The trip to her house was not easy. We started out by car taxi, then switched to bicycle taxi and finally traveled by foot along a dusty path. As we moved through the area, curious people began to follow us. By the time we arrived at a little house, we had close to 50 of them trailing us. We had an interpreter with us; the parents were very nice and gave me tea and a small chair to sit on. I looked outside and saw an open sewer. I had a hard time drinking the tea.

The little girl, Bui Thi Huyen, was six years old and had never moved by herself. She sat, terrified and crying, on an old pile of rags. I gave her lollipops but that did not seem to help. We put her in the wheelchair outside her house, where our followers had gathered. I showed her how to put her hands on the wheel rims to move the chair. She was frightened and tearful. But finally, she moved it by herself. Then she broke out into the biggest smile I have ever seen (see for yourself in the picture in this book). All of her neighbors clapped and cheered. In a few moments, we had transformed this girl on a pile of rags into a girl who could move about freely. The gift of a wheelchair had opened up a new life to her. She could now go to school and build a future. She had found a new world.

We made the long trip back to Hanoi, where we continued to distribute wheelchairs. Many of the wheelchair recipients were victims of land mines, farming accidents, Agent Orange and war. Others had birth defects. They ranged in age from young children to the elderly. They had little in life, but they were resourceful in managing their disabilities. Their stories and dreams moved us.

One woman arrived carrying on her back a boy almost as big as she was. He had cerebral palsy. We were taking pictures of recipients as they received their wheelchairs. When it was time for the boy's picture, the mother said, "Wait a minute." She started grooming her son for the picture. She wiped his face with a rag, combed his hair and arranged his clothes. She wanted him to look as good as possible. It was a lesson in unconditional love. I could see how much she cared for her son, no matter how difficult it was to support him.

An elderly lady came to me to thank me for her wheelchair. She told me that she was 78 years old. Her teeth were black and broken. She told me that because of her immobility, she had wanted to die. Then she took my hands, came close, smiled and said, "But now I don't want to."

I met a 17-year-old girl who was unable to walk but was the top student in her class. She dreamed of being a doctor. But she was afraid that she wouldn't be able to continue her education because of her inability to get around. To that point in her life, she had to be carried by family or friends wherever she needed to go. I'll never forget her expression of sheer joy and gratitude when she received her wheelchair. Now she would be able to fulfill her dream and attend medical school.

The wheelchair helped not only her but also her family and friends, who no longer had to carry her. Wheelchairs not only improve the lives of recipients, they also change the lives of the people who care for them. We estimate that each wheelchair delivered improved the quality of at least 10 lives—parents, siblings, friends and caregivers.

At the end of the distribution, we still had 10 wheelchairs left. We decided to take them to the hospital doctor who had helped us with customs. We figured some of his patients could use them. After we arrived, we gave out the wheelchairs and took pictures with the recipients. As we were leaving, someone came to us and said that there was a problem: there were three people in the back of the room who thought they were going to get a wheelchair but did not. These people were crying and inconsolable.

I went to the back. They were the leprosy patients that I had spoken to earlier. They'd heard we were returning to the hospital. Because I had visited them earlier, they were convinced they were going to receive wheelchairs. It was the first time in their lives that they had hoped for something, and now that hope was gone. I talked to them and tried to quiet them; I told them I would try to help. We had no more chairs to give, but I would not be the one to dash their hopes.

We drove through the town, desperately searching for more wheelchairs. After several hours, we finally located three used ones.

I bought them and brought them back to the hospital. I've never seen anyone as grateful as these forgotten people when we placed them in the wheelchairs. They lived in one tiny room together, with nowhere to go and only each other to look at. Leprosy had robbed them of their freedom and dignity. Now they could go outside and sit in the sun, a simple thing that made a world of difference to them.

I returned to the U.S. filled with a sense of achievement.

After Vietnam, Hope Haven asked me to help on other distributions. We did a big one in Guatemala in April 2000. I agreed to pay for the wheelchairs and helped organize the trip there.

We drove to a warehouse in a distant village to distribute some of them. As I was entering, I saw a man being carried in. He was in great pain and I could see that his leg was swollen. I went to him with an interpreter and asked him what had happened. He said that he had been hurt while working in a field. I asked, "Have you seen a doctor?" He said, "Yes. They had a doctor look at my leg and he said I had gangrene and that I needed to get the leg taken off in the next 30 days or I will die."

The man asked if we could loan him a wheelchair so he could try to borrow the money for surgery. He said, "The doctor wants $100 to cut off my leg and another $25 if he has to put me to sleep during the operation. If I can't get the money, I will have my family bring the wheelchair back to you."

I was speechless. Looking at him in his pain, I counted out $125 and handed it to him. He was in shock. He could not believe someone was helping him. The man looked at the money and counted it. Then he handed me back $25 and said he did not have to be asleep for the operation. I gave the money back to him and assured him that I wanted him to be put to sleep. About four days later, he had a nun call to thank me and to let me know that his leg was removed successfully and he was already using the wheelchair. His wife had found a new job and he was going to take care of the house and children. The nun said that the family was happy once again.

It's difficult to describe my reaction to this encounter. I was horrified imagining what this man would have gone through had I not been there to help.

We also met an American nurse during the trip. She'd spent most of her life in Guatemala trying to help the poor. She was something else. It's hard for me to imagine completely changing your life that way, giving up everything and focusing only on helping the least fortunate. To me, doing that kind of work constantly would knock you down, depress you. I loved my experience in Guatemala, but I knew I could return to the life I've always lived. As I said in the previous chapter, I personally feel the need to effect change on a larger scale, to help as many people as I can instead of just a few, like this nurse. But she told me she had never been happier. She'd found something that gave her complete satisfaction—a purpose in life. I admired her for that. She inspired me.

The nurse led us to another very poor part of the city, to a tiny shack where we met a couple with a little girl. She was about six or seven years old, and she was sitting in a small box. Her mother said she had to work during the day so she couldn't care for her daughter. The little girl had to stay in the box most of the day. The child didn't know what it was like to move on her own. She couldn't go to school, go outside or even feel the breeze on her face. It seemed like the most miserable existence I could imagine. When we gave her a wheelchair, her mother was incredibly grateful. She told us that for the first time, her child would be able to move around the house. It would allow her to go to school and receive an education. No longer would she be condemned to a box. She would have a future.

We completed our distributions in Guatemala and returned to the U.S. The people I'd met on my trips had told me tragic stories. They left a lasting impression on me. I realized that there are many people in the world whose lives can be transformed in a simple way.

A wheelchair gave them independence and mobility. I had witnessed it firsthand.

But the trips gave me something, too. I've never been an emotional person. But the simple act of giving had allowed me to open my heart. I felt truly needed for the first time in my life, and it was a great feeling. By the time I arrived home from Guatemala, I was certain I'd found the purpose I'd been searching for.

I researched the worldwide need for wheelchairs. It was pretty clear that millions of people in many countries could use them and couldn't afford them. A good basic wheelchair today costs about $500 in the U.S.; a more advanced one costs hundreds of dollars more. In some countries, that can equal the income for a family for an entire year. No one else was giving away wheelchairs, so why shouldn't I?

It would be a huge undertaking. But I was never one to back down from a challenge. I decided to create a nonprofit organization to deliver wheelchairs wherever they were needed, without regard to race, religion, politics or nationality. I wanted to reach as many people as possible. My team got to work.

At a press conference in June 2000, we announced the creation of the Wheelchair Foundation. Our goal: to distribute one million free wheelchairs. We estimated the cost at more than $150 million. I pledged $15 million to the effort through my personal foundation. Others could contribute $75 to sponsor a wheelchair and we'd deliver it (the cost has since risen to $150 due to increased expenses, but that is still a bargain price for a wheelchair to be donated). Our international board of advisors soon included King Juan Carlos, Mikhail Gorbachev and Nelson Mandela. Our new partners included LDS Charities and other humanitarian organizations. It was the beginning of a mission that would fulfill me in ways that I had never imagined.

I was now passionate about the difference wheelchairs could

make in a person's life. The need was enormous. An estimated 100 million or more people around the world need a wheelchair and most cannot afford one. I knew I'd have to raise a lot of money and enlist the support of many others to reach my goals. But I willingly accepted the challenge. Like Theodore Roosevelt's "man in the arena," I felt great devotion and great enthusiasm for a worthy cause.

I had found joy. I had found purpose.

Now, more than a decade later, the Wheelchair Foundation has helped millions of recipients, their families and donors find joy and purpose, too, and helped turn some into leaders. There are countless stories to tell about them.

Let me start with Josh Routh and his dad, Don.

At a wheelchair distribution in Nicaragua in 2007, Josh brought a bright new red wheelchair in a van to a frail, thin man in a remote village. Josh also gave him a custom foam knee wedge, which the disabled person inserts between his knees to help prevent chafing that can occur to unprotected legs.

As the wheelchair distribution team prepared to depart, a boy knocked on the van door, took a gold bracelet from his wrist and handed it to Josh. The boy was the son of the frail man Josh had given the wheelchair and knee wedge to; the son wanted to give Josh his most prized possession to show his appreciation and love. The two hugged and cried. Josh now wears the bracelet from time-to-time and keeps it in a special place in his home. That memory has remained in Josh's heart.

For that knee wedge was not an extra piece of equipment the distribution team brought with it—it was Josh's own. Josh himself uses a wheelchair. Born with cerebral palsy, Josh, 33, has been in a wheelchair since he was four. Doctors said he would be a quadriplegic and never be able to talk. But with years of physical therapy and a good education, Josh grew strong and flourished—even excelling at wheelchair basketball and other sports. A wheelchair is so much a part of him that he never thinks about it, nor does his family. It has allowed him to live a full, independent life, with his own house, car and job. He is the most popular cashier at Nob Hill Foods, a grocery store in San Ramon, California, his hometown. Josh's life is about ability, not disability.

But Josh's story does not end there. Despite his disability, Josh and his dad are two of our most committed volunteers. Josh and Don have dedicated their lives to helping people with physical challenges, distributing more than 5,000 wheelchairs on 15 trips to 11 countries in Latin America since 2006. Initially, Don and Josh got help in funding from the Rotary Club of North Pleasanton, California. Now they are expanding their fundraising activities to local schools. Their "third wheel" is Rotarian Bill Wheeler, a successful businessman and wheelchair volunteer since 2001. Rotarians in the U.S. and worldwide are among our biggest supporters. But talk about commitment: despite Josh's physical challenges, Josh and Don have promised contributors that they will personally put recipients into their new wheelchairs on site.

How dedicated is Josh to this promise and work? One time, in Panama in 2008, they promised to deliver just two wheelchairs to an indigenous tribe of about 150 people. The only way to get to their village was down a river in the jungle in a dugout canoe. They traveled during a driving rainstorm with Josh's wheelchair strapped to the bow of the canoe. The tribe lived in open-air huts built on stilts on top of a plateau maybe 150 feet above the intersection of two rivers. A welcoming party of several men in loincloths met them. Four barefoot men picked up Josh in his wheelchair and carried him up the side of the small mountain on a rain-slicked, moss-covered dirt path (see the pictures in this book!). After spending several hours and sharing a meal of fish and plantains, the Chief gave Josh his knife made of bone. The tribesmen carried Josh back down the mountain and they headed home in the rain.

When Josh and Don talk about what this kind of experience has given them, their eyes well up with tears.

"We were so fortunate and blessed to be living here and Josh to be born here and having access to everything he needed that having a wheelchair was never a consideration—there was never any doubt of whether Josh was going to have a wheelchair," Don said. "Then you stop and think about 100 million people that don't even have access to a wheelchair, where a wheelchair is an unaffordable luxury for them. That's what's so important to us as givers—we want to give these people as much opportunity as possible for them to lead a normal life and have mobility, because we feel so blessed that Josh had the opportunities he had here…. It's allowed me to give back. And that's the greatest feeling of all. And that's what this is all about—being able to do something that has an impact on society."

"Helping other people is very special to me because I understand how it is to be in a wheelchair. I have freedom and dignity with my wheelchair," Josh said. "It makes my heart happy when I am able to help somebody who has a disability like me but has no wheelchair to get around. I feel fortunate and I want to share with others."

Thank you Josh and Don. And thank you for your leadership.

Giving to others does not just make you feel good, it can also help heal—sometimes not just the recipient, but also the donor.

In November 2006, the Vietnam Veterans of Diablo Valley, California, traveled to South Vietnam, where some of them had fought more than 40 years ago. They were returning on a mission of peace and goodwill instead of war and destruction. During their 13-day distribution trip, vets and volunteers gave away 560 wheelchairs to disabled Vietnamese. The veterans had spent two years collecting the funds needed for the donations. Their return to Vietnam was as much an opportunity to aid those in need as it was to mend part of themselves—a chance to find closure, create new memories, and replace enemies with friends. Their first distribution was in Ho Chi Minh City (formerly Saigon). Over the next hour, the veterans gave away many wheelchairs.

"I think that most of us were not prepared to see such physical and mental need among these people, and our first tears were shed," said John Estes, U.S. Marine Corps (retired). "But this was just the beginning."

In Quy Nhon the next day, the group got to see firsthand how the team's helping hands affected the daily lives of those in need of a wheelchair. Whole families were there to see their children, grandparents, and moms and dads receive something that would completely change their lives for the better. They cried and the vets cried with them. They laughed and they laughed with them.

In Quy Nhon, they met a wonderful woman named Nguyen Nga who, with the help of some of her handicapped students, educated, fed and cared for nearly 200 disabled orphans every day. Proud of her kids, she introduced the veterans to her staff. It was there, Estes said, that he was struck by the enormity of the need of the Vietnamese people. He reached down to shake the hand of one office helper and saw that she did not have a hand. He forced a smile but was speechless.

At Kids First Village in Dong Ha a few days later, the team distributed wheelchairs and 60 lbs. of medicine. When "Wild Bill" LaVigne, U.S. Army (retired) helped a beautiful young girl into her new wheelchair and made her smile, he and Rich Vannucci, U.S. Navy (retired), began to weep.

In Hanoi on their last day, these ex-military men visited the Vietnam Friendship Village. Along with disabled children, the center cares for some old soldiers. There, nearly 40 years after the U.S. war in Vietnam ended, the veterans came face-to-face with some of their fellow warriors, men whom they'd faced in combat so long ago.

Through interpreters, they told each other stories, they hugged and shook hands. They found out just how much they were alike. They parted with a promise to return.

"We came, we saw, we laughed and we cried. We gave some, but we got back much, much more. And we changed," Estes said.

On their last day in Vietnam, Skip George, U.S. Army Special Forces (retired), said, "There are two kinds of people in this world, those that do and those that don't." Well, with the help of those at the Wheelchair Foundation, his group "did."

That is leadership.

For some people and businesses, giving is a good investment. Because he is a businessman, Val Nunes tries to get a good return on every investment he makes, including sponsoring wheelchair donations.

"I want a good return on the money I donate to Wheelchair Foundation. What else are you going to do with $150 that will have such a big impact on someone else's life?" Val said. "And a wheelchair is a life-changing investment!"

Val and his wife, Belia, of Oakland, California, have supported Wheelchair Foundation for more than a decade and have traveled to more than 15 countries around the world to distribute wheelchairs. Years ago, they were part of the core group of volunteers who started Wine for Wheels (www.wineforwheels. org), which they both actively support and use as a model to get others involved.

"It's a way of coming together with people for a common cause and contributing to something positive," said Val, who is the vice president of sales at Dreisbach, a refrigerated logistics company in Oakland, California. He encouraged his company and business partners to get involved with Wheelchair Foundation. This led to a partnership between Dole Foods, Dreisbach and Wine for Wheels, and provided hundreds of new wheelchairs to the people of the Philippines in 2008.

That is leadership.

One of the recipients who came to the Philippine distribution rolled up on a plank of wood with wheels on it. He addressed the crowd at the distribution and said he was 45 years old and had been rolling around on that piece of wood for 30 years. And for the very first time he was able "to sit up and feel like a man." He told the distribution team about all the places he could not go before he got his new wheelchair because he couldn't access them with his plank with wheels on it. Val told him that it was a shame that he had to wait 30 years for someone to help him out and he pledged to send more wheelchairs for the Filipino people. The Dole executives who hosted and participated in the distribution would later say it was "the greatest thing that we have been able to do for the people of our community!"

"Our experiences have given us so much in return for our work," Val said. "When you go out and help people, there is a part of you that knows when you help someone, you are doing something good—but you also give of yourself. And you sacrifice some of yourself in doing so. One of the most valuable lessons I have ever learned came from Ken Behring. He told us, 'Give, and get involved. A smile is reward enough for your efforts, and the act of giving is in itself a gift.' He is right, and we are always motivated to do more."

Come with me now around the world to learn about the work of other donors, volunteers and recipients—and leaders in all three groups.

Chapter 9:
WHEELCHAIRS AROUND THE WORLD

Never doubt that a small group of thoughtful, committed citizens can change the world. Indeed, it is the only thing that ever has.

Margaret Mead

In the years since I founded the Wheelchair Foundation, I have participated in hundreds of wheelchair distributions and have had thousands of moving experiences. I've met remarkable individuals who somehow managed to endure in a world that offered them little hope or meaning. I have watched their lives suddenly become transformed by a simple gift that gave them independence and mobility.

In the two weeks after our press conference in Washington, DC, in 2000, we received requests for 160,000 wheelchairs from non-governmental organizations (NGOs) that do philanthropic work all over the world. From the beginning, we have relied heavily on our partners to meet this demand. Our first partner was The Church of Jesus Christ of Latter-day Saints. After launching the Foundation, we worked closely with the church's humanitarian arm, LDS Charities, to distribute tens of thousands of wheelchairs around the world.

In 2001, we entered into a global relationship with Rotary Clubs, combining funds to deliver wheelchairs throughout the world. This partnership allows us to deliver a shipping container of 280 wheelchairs (a container is the size of an 18-wheel truck) to just about anywhere in the world for $42,000, or $150 per wheelchair. We soon adopted this program as our official way of combining resources to reach more people in need.

In the following pages, I write about some of places we have visited, the many people we have met and the joy we have experienced in helping them. We helped changed their lives—and our donors and volunteers agree that they changed ours.

"Lift them from the ground and offer them a life," said Mike Hoffman, a doctor, after a distribution in Mexico in 2009. "The life you change will likely be your own."

"I wasn't prepared for the emotional impact," Steven Lloyd said after a trip to distribute wheelchairs in Serbia in 2011. "The instant gratification of actually helping people into their brand new beautiful wheelchairs—it makes you want to give more and more."

"I am different after having the experience of giving personally and directly," said Jennifer Davis after a 2011 distribution in Guatemala. "To touch another human life at such a great level is—awesome! It will be an honor to give again."

AFRICA

After my business success, I decided I was ready to travel the world. In Africa, I met many people without hope, freedom and dignity because they were physically disabled and did not have the money to deal with their immobility. It was the first place I delivered humanitarian supplies and where I first found a purpose.

Zimbabwe

At a distribution in this country in southern Africa, one of the first people we met was a man who had crawled 12 miles on his elbows to come to the distribution. Once in a wheelchair, he started pushing himself around and around. After about an hour of using it, he pulled himself out and sat back on the ground. I asked him through an interpreter, "Why did you get out of the wheelchair?"

"I've had my turn," he said. "Twenty years ago, I had my turn in a wheelchair, too. That is the reason I came back today—so I could have another turn to move myself."

Shocked, I told him, "No, this is your wheelchair."

"I have no money," he said. "It cannot be my wheelchair because I have no money to buy it."

"No, you don't need any money," I said. "We brought this wheelchair for you. It is a gift." He was overjoyed and thankful.

A year later, we went back to the same area for another distribution. The same man was there in his wheelchair; several children surrounded him. "I came back 12 miles," he said, "because I want to show you that the wheelchair is just like new and my children here want to thank you for what you have done for me."

At that distribution, the staff asked me to talk to a young man who had carried a woman for two days and two nights so she could get a wheelchair. I asked him through an interpreter, "Is she your mother?"

He said, "No."

"Is she your relative?"

"No."

"Is she your close friend?"

"No."

"Then why did you carry her for so long to get her here for a wheelchair?"

He said, "She asked me to. Now look at how happy she is. So it was worthwhile." His simple explanation said it all.

South Africa

We have distributed more than 22,000 wheelchairs in South Africa. We made one young lady happy on a special day.

"Two years ago, you were here. You were giving wheelchairs away and I was not lucky enough to get one." She added, "Every day and night for two years, I have prayed to God that He would bring you back to bring me a wheelchair. Today, after two years, God sent you back with a wheelchair for me." Then she told us, "And today is my birthday."

In August 2001, we met in Johannesburg with Nelson Mandela, who was a member of our International Board of Advisors. He had been sick and was going for chemotherapy that afternoon. We spent the morning with him. We talked about world events and his life experiences. Because of his illness, we arranged for our distribution to take place at his house. When the wheelchair recipients arrived, Mandela met with each one and gave each child a kiss. I saw for myself what a great man he is and how much he cares for the people of South Africa.

At the press conference after the distribution, Mandela said, "I am very happy that Mr. Behring has been so generous in bringing us these wheelchairs." Then, looking at me, he said, "It is one thing to ask for help, but when someone comes to you on his own and gives you something without asking for anything in return, this is a sign of true friendship for the people of South Africa."

In July 2003, I had the honor of being one of the guests at Mandela's 85th birthday party, along with former President Bill Clinton and his wife, former senator and Secretary of State Hillary Clinton, and many celebrities.

Botswana

In many African countries, making handmade crafts or clothing is vital to the local economy. During a distribution in Botswana, I met a young woman, about 20 years old. She crawled to us with a piece of leather strapped around her knees and lower body. The leather held in thin, wiry legs—because of poor water quality, she had been born with a birth defect. Her legs had not formed properly. We gave her a wheelchair, but I will never forget her eyes—she had lifeless eyes.

After the distribution, the local people took me to a sewing shop. Across the room, I saw somebody waving at me. It was the young woman. She wheeled the chair to me all by herself and her face beamed with joy. She told me that for the first time, she could learn how to make clothes! She could now make a living! I couldn't believe what I was seeing—the very same day this woman had received a wheelchair, she had received a new life. And there is nothing more rewarding.

Angola

A delivery team traveled on another mission to Angola in 2002. It met a group of physically disabled men who were visiting the capital, Luanda, for a wheelchair basketball tournament. They planned to play in borrowed wheelchairs. Each young man had a unique story of how he had lost the use of his legs: one in a farming accident, one in a motorcycle accident, one to a land mine. The team arranged to have wheelchairs delivered to their village so they wouldn't have to crawl to and from school, church and their homes.

"I want to thank you for the wheelchair you are giving me," one of the young men said. "My father ignores me because my disability makes him look bad to other people in my village. The only time that he is proud of me is when I am in a wheelchair playing basketball." The young man paused and could not hold back his emotion. As tears began to form in his eyes, he sat up straight and said to me, "Now my father will be proud of me all of the time, and that makes me very, very happy."

Ghana

In Ghana in 2011, in the city of Accra, our team spoke to a group of disabled young men about life in their country without a wheelchair. A young disabled man quietly asked our team, "What is a wheelchair?" Yes, in some parts of the world in the 21st century, people in poverty have never heard of or seen a wheelchair.

One of our most devoted contributors and volunteers, Gordon Holmes, helped with the answer. He is the owner of Lookout Ridge Winery in Kenwood, California. Around the time he started the winery, Gordon's wife, Kari, was diagnosed with multiple sclerosis. Eventually, she needed a wheelchair to get around. After I met Gordon at a wine event, he got involved and eventually helped to found Wine for Wheels, one of our support programs built around social events. For every bottle of Lookout Ridge Current Release Wines a customer buys from Gordon, and for every case of Library Wines purchased, Lookout Ridge donates a wheelchair in the customer's name.

"We believe you can buy a bottle and change a life," Gordon said.

He did for that young man in Accra.

CHINA

When I first started going to the Far East in the 1960s, I spent time in Taiwan, Hong Kong and South Korea. China was not ready for people like me. But I wanted to go there. I was fascinated by the country and felt I could get close to its culture.

By geography, China is the fourth largest country in the world. But it has the biggest population, more than 1.3 billion citizens.

As one of the world's oldest civilizations, China's written history goes back 4,000 years. There is always a lot to explore, from the imperial palaces to cave sculpture, martial arts to calligraphy, noodles to Chinese opera. When you get close and try to understand the culture, you will find a certain connection; it reflects the same humanity that is found everywhere in this world. China remains a place of contrasts: the rice paddies of farmers in the countryside; Shanghai's skyscrapers; Starbucks and McDonald's opening their outlets in historic sites in Beijing; rickshaws and taxies competing for tourists in small towns.

My first trip to China was in 1978, to explore business opportunities. At that time, the people dressed only in black, gray or dark blue clothes. The disastrous Cultural Revolution had just come to an end, leaving buildings covered with slogans and posters. The people seemed numb and confused. They earned little, and there was little for them to buy in shops. Foreigners were rarely seen in the streets, but wherever they were, they received a lot of attention and hospitality.

In fact, some big changes were taking place that year. As a visitor, I could not see much beyond the society's surface. But what happened next is beyond anyone's imagination. That year, the government started opening China to foreign trade and investment. China began its transition from a centrally-planned economy to a more market-oriented one. As a result of those reforms, the country's gross domestic product has increased more than 30-fold, making it the second largest economy in the world. China has become the exciting and dynamic country we see today.

I now fly to China about four times a year. I usually land in Shanghai or Beijing, then travel to other cities and towns. Everywhere I go, I see construction sites: old buildings being torn down to make room for new buildings, roads and gardens. There are more and more new cars and buses and migrant workers, making the cities feel even more crowded. There is also a growing middle class, which enjoys such luxuries as the new televisions and mobile phones. These new consumers do not have go far to find the latest fashions from Paris or the latest electronic gadgets from Japan. And in their small home offices, they follow stocks in Chinese companies like Sina or Sohu as closely as any American investor follows Apple or Google.

China is such a big country—9.6 million square kilometers—that its cities and towns are very different from one another in style, customs and living standards. Shanghai is the most dynamic city, perhaps in the world. It has an amazing skyline formed by scores of skyscrapers across the east and west banks of the Huangpu River. It is a city full of energy and opportunity. Like New York City, it is a melting pot, from expatriates to businesspeople from Hong Kong and Taiwan to local Shanghaiese and laborers from the rural west. Ever on the lookout for new ventures and seeing the rising wealth of China, I am an investor in a high-end golf community with custom mansions and villas on Chongming Island on the outskirts of Shanghai. It is called "The Sanctuary at Dongtan" and is set in the island's spectacular natural locations.

Beijing, the capital city, is more political. It's full of officials from the domestic and foreign governments and is the headquarters for many foreign companies that operate in China. There are a lot of historic and scenic spots in Beijing, making it a prime destination for tourists.

Each location offers its own beauty. But one thing they have in common is the people. I love Chinese people. They are some of the friendliest, smartest, most hardworking people I have ever met. Since we began distributing wheelchairs in China, I have made many friends there. One of the things that impresses me about the Chinese is their hospitality and the way they show their appreciation. Wherever you go in China, the local citizens always share their best with you—their food, their homes, their facilities. They spend time and effort to communicate with you and try to understand your culture. In fact, studying English, the international language of business, is now mandatory in many schools. Chinese people are also diligent and talented. More often than not, I meet physically disabled people in China who are good singers, painters or craftspeople. And those who work for the benefit of the physically disabled prove their worth and capability. In all, people are the energy of this country and the driving force behind making China so successful.

Because of its size, China most likely has the largest population of physically disabled people of any country in the world. The China Disabled Persons' Federation (CDPF) estimates that 8.8 million Chinese are physically disabled; other estimates run as high as 35 million. The government is very aware of their challenges—in 1991, it declared "the third Sunday of May every year shall be designated as the National Day of Supporting Persons with Disabilities." No matter what the number, most immobile Chinese don't have the funds to buy a wheelchair. As a result, we have made a major commitment to distribute wheelchairs in China.

To begin with, we purchase our wheelchairs from four factories there. This has made my feelings for the Chinese people even stronger and given me a greater appreciation of their capabilities.

We started meeting local politicians and party leaders. In 2001, we established a partnership with the CDPF. It has been a significant and effective partnership, because the work of the CDPF makes delivering wheelchairs to the neediest in China most efficient. In China, almost every immobile person is registered with the organization, which keeps detailed records of their health and status. Through the CDPF, we get a better idea of who needs help. Together, we deliver wheelchairs city by city and town by town.

The CDPF was started by Deng Pufang, the son of China's late president, Deng Xiaoping. He is a well-recognized figure in China, not only because of his special background, but also because of his commitment to the millions of people in China who are physically disabled. In 1968, during the Cultural Revolution, Pufang was pushed off a balcony and broke his back. He has used a wheelchair since that day. He told me that the highs and lows of his life have committed him to humanitarian work in his country. He has established a chapter of the CDPF in every major city in China. For his work, he has received numerous awards, including the Lions Clubs International Award. The Rotarians honored him with a Paul Harris Fellowship. The United Nations has named him one of its Messengers of Peace. His journey has made him a true leader.

In 2003, we entered into a partnership with the Chinese Ministry of Civil Affairs to deliver 52,000 wheelchairs to rural areas. In 2004, we teamed with the China Charity Federation to start a program called "Operation Mobility." It solicits donations from companies doing business in China, which will be eligible for tax deductions for sponsoring wheelchairs. So far, the program has funded more than 55,000 free wheelchairs.

Since beginning our distributions in China in 2001, we have distributed more than 325,000 wheelchairs in more than 40 cities and towns, including 500 wheelchairs to the victims of the Tang Shan earthquake that occurred in Hebei province in 1976. It killed hundreds of thousands of people and left tens of thousands immobile. Our distribution day was the 25th anniversary of the earthquake. With local leaders, we gave out the wheelchairs, all of which went to people who had been in bed for 25 years. I shook hands with each of the recipients. Everyone was overcome with emotion.

Each of our donation ceremonies in China is well organized and attended by government officials, volunteers and media representatives. No matter how many recipients there are, I try to shake hands with every one. They are often so happy to receive a wheelchair that they grab my hands tightly and, with tears in their eyes, they smile, because I've told them all I want in return from them is a smile.

In spring 2004, we went to Shenyang to distribute 1,000 wheelchairs. It was a beautiful day. When I arrived at the city square, I couldn't believe my eyes: before me were 1,000 physically disabled people sitting in 1,000 wheelchairs, all of them dressed in red T-shirts and white caps. As a children's band played marching songs, volunteers dressed in the same T-shirts and caps stood in line, waiting to help. Many happy family members and passersby looked on. I gave a short speech, as did a couple of local officials. Then we went down to shake hands with each recipient. That is my routine: I give them a wheelchair, my hand and a smile, along with expressing the love and affection of the people of the United States.

At the distribution, I met Wu Li. Immobile from the age of nine months (she contracted polio), Li could not go to school. But she never gave up. She educated herself and taught herself English from watching television and listening to the radio. When she got her wheelchair, she said, "I can go to a bookstore, market and any place I like. I can study at school or take some training courses."

She went on to say, "I cannot thank Mr. Behring more. He knows what we need most. He has given us mobility. Now we can study, live, work, make friends and contribute to our country."

Then she said, profoundly, "A disabled person plus a wheelchair equals a healthy person." It is an equation that I will never forget. Something that simple means so much.

On another trip, I heard the story of a severely physically disabled baby with birth defects who was abandoned in a shopping center in 1993. The police investigated but couldn't find the parents, so they took the baby no one wanted to the Kunshan Orphanage. The staff there named him Kun Sha. By the time he reached the age of two, Sha's condition had improved slightly, but he was still unable to stand on his own. The Amity Foundation in Hong Kong learned of Sha and funded operations on his fingers, ankles, elbows and knees in 1995 and again in 1997. The orphanage developed a special training program to help Sha recover from his many surgeries.

Two years passed as Sha continued to stretch muscles and ligaments in his determination to walk. With the aid of crutches, he was finally able to do so in 1999. In 2000, Sha began school, where the same spirit and desire to succeed that marked his physical progress drove him to earn good grades and live as normal a life as possible. In 2002, a team from the Wheelchair Foundation made Sha's life even better by presenting him with a wheelchair. I was particularly impressed with Sha, who sang a song at the distribution ceremony titled "Little Boy Seeking Dad." It went:

Not afraid of raining, not afraid of snowing.
I only want to find him, even if it's cold and windy
    and snowy.
I want to see him every day, my Dad;
I'm going to find my Daddy,
    no matter what outside looks like.
I'm going to find my Daddy,
To find my Daddy, no matter where he is.
I can't find my dearest Daddy;
If you find him, please ask him to come back home.

He sang in a glorious voice. The song drove home the point of what it feels like not only to be disabled, but to be abandoned. As he sat next to me, he looked into my eyes and asked me, "Are you my grandfather?" I would have loved to have been able to say "yes." I was very pleased that we were able to give Sha a new wheelchair and help make his life easier and more enjoyable. I also gave the orphanage $1,000 for his education. After several more surgeries in recent years, Kun Sha can now walk on his own! He no longer needs a wheelchair or cane. He graduated from junior high school in 2012 and enrolled in a five-year high school associate degree program. He is very happy.

This is how $150 (for a wheelchair) can save a human being.

Other wheelchair recipients have amazed me. We gave Xie Yan-hong from Dalian a wheelchair in 2003. He was born without the use of his legs. He used his wheelchair to accelerate an ambitious exercise program. He swam great distances every day to strengthen his upper body. When I returned to China in 2004, he told me he had used his wheelchair to travel to England, where he became the first physically disabled person ever to swim the English Channel! He swam 21 miles from England to France in 16 hours and 44 minutes.

He later wrote me the following letter:

Dear Respectable Mr. Behring,

This is the second time I meet you. Last year, when we first met from the wheelchair donation ceremony, I didn't realize what a gift you've brought to me until today. I know it is not only a wheelchair, but also you've brought a blessing, a good luck to me!

Sitting on the wheelchair you gave to me, I went to the English Channel and successfully swam across over this channel. The challenge is huge. But with the great encouragement from you dear Mr. Behring and with tremendous help and support from my disabled friends, from Dalian CDPF and Dalian government leaders Mr. Xia, I became the first disabled person to meet this challenge and I won! It's your love brought to me the success. If I could, I dream some day I can go to U.S. and challenge to swim across the channel in U.S. again. I want to tell the world I am able!

Thank you for your love! I will cherish your love and keep it in my heart for always!

Xie Yanhong

This is what wheelchairs and a simple act of giving can do for people.

At another delivery, Lin Yu Liang was a recipient. Mr. Lin also suffered from polio. As a child, his parents carried him to school. They gave him a small wooden stool that he rocked from side to side to move himself, but he mainly stayed at home and dreamed of a normal life. We gave Mr. Lin a wheelchair and later learned that he went back to his village and opened a small "milk bar." Not only that, he got married! He was proud of the fact that he was the only physically disabled businessman in his village. His wheelchair helped him become a leader! He kept his stool but bragged, "I forgot how to use it."

At a distribution in Shanghai, I met a young man who was paralyzed from the neck down. But he was a fabulous painter—he painted with a brush in his mouth. In gratitude for receiving a wheelchair, he painted me a beautiful picture of a peacock. I think it is the most incredible thing I have ever seen. I was amazed at his ability to paint so many colors in such a small area. This treasure is now on display in our Wheelchair Foundation gallery in Danville, California.

Not even the severe acute respiratory syndrome (SARS) scare could keep me away from these wonderful people. SARS is a serious respiratory illness that researchers believe originated in the Far East after 2000; it killed hundreds of people there. But while the West was shunning China, I traveled there. Physically disabled people were depending on me and I was not going to let them down. My trip was written up in national newspapers. Such volunteerism is a concept foreign to many Chinese, and they try to understand the motivation. I tell them it's simple: I get more in return from being here with you than you get from being here with me. And I tell them that the wheelchairs are not just a gift from me, but from many wonderful people in the U.S.

They are beginning to understand.

In Shanghai in 2012, about 20 employees of Qualcomm, the mobile technology company, met 10 physically disabled people in Gongqing Forest Park. The employees are members of the company's "QCare" volunteer team. They brought 10 wheelchairs to the park that day to give to recipients; together, they played games and had lunch.

It was all new to Qualcomm administrative manager Sharon Qin, who was not sure what to expect. The Foundation staff had provided some pre-event training to Sharon and her colleagues, but Sharon had not had much exposure to physically disabled people. She was partnered with a 50-year-old-man. At one moment during the game, the man turned and looked up from his new red wheelchair to the nervous Sharon—and gave her some support.

"The score is not important," she recalled him saying, putting her at ease. "Let's just have fun."

Sharon had assumed the man was unhappy because of his disability, his circumstances. But in that moment, she learned that he was happy—and that other physically disabled people, on their own or with the support of family, friends and community, can be, too. "I learned about sharing happiness with others," she added. "I refreshed my values and thought about how to be happier myself. I want to participate in more of these kinds of activities."

Sharon had answered the call of her colleague Susan Yang, a senior human resources officer in Qualcomm's Shanghai office. Part of Susan's job was to manage company community outreach and improvement efforts in the office. After Susan learned of the Foundation on the Internet, she convinced her company to use part of its outreach budget to sponsor 300 wheelchairs. Susan helped recruit fellow Qualcomm employees to distribute them throughout the city. Sharon was one such volunteer. Together, they established Wheelchair Day for the Shanghai office and its workers.

Both Susan and Sharon had to make independent evaluations of the Wheelchair Foundation as a non-profit. After doing the research, both women were able to wholeheartedly recommend the Foundation as a good nonprofit partner for Qualcomm. They said our Foundation had a "good track record" in China and that our staff members did an "impressive" job and were "very professional." Wheelchair Day was a "great way to give back to society," Susan said—and great for the company's teambuilding efforts.

"Most the people they want to do good things and also as an employer we also want to give the employees this kind of a chance. I just realized everyone on our team, each member they truly enjoyed their time at the event," Susan said. "So as an organizer I feel happy to see this kind of outcome. I also feel happy that I helped others. And I kind of get the chance to become closer with the whole team, the other departments."

And this kind of effort takes leadership.

Our work has been welcomed in China. At a dinner in 2001, the mayor of Shanghai told me, "We did not ask you to come here. You came here because you wanted to help our people. You came here with no strings attached. That is true friendship."

But the needs of the physically disabled will only grow in China as its population ages. One expert at Peking University in Beijing told me that by 2050, more than 80 million Chinese will be over the age of 80 and many will be immobile

Our philanthropic work in China is increasing beyond wheelchairs. One exciting area we are working on is clean water technology. Through the Global Health and Education Foundation's Safe

Water Drinking Project, we are working with Chinese universities researching technology for producing pure water at low cost to the entire world. During the 20th century, the world's population tripled but water use multiplied six times. According to the United Nations, almost 1.1 billion people have inadequate access to clean water and 2.6 billion are without appropriate sanitation. As a result, approximately 1.8 million people die every year from diarrheal disease, and astonishingly 90 percent of those deaths occur in children under the age of five. We must develop a comprehensive approach to providing safe water to today's children, ensuring that they will not only have a chance to survive, but also to grow into leaders who understand and appreciate the value of public health, sustainable health and economic development and, most importantly, human dignity.

Through our Safe Drinking Water Project in China, we are working with local governments and departments, selecting suitable locations and carrying out feasibility studies, purchasing water purification systems, overseeing water station construction and sanitation quality control, as well as conducting public health and sanitation education in rural areas to help eliminate waterborne diseases and impurities.

We started a pilot project in Shanyin County, Shanxi province of China, where the water includes high levels of fluoride and arsenic. (In my trips to Africa, I have seen tribal people in Kenya and Tanzania, the Maasai, crippled and killed by too much of these in their drinking water.) We selected an appropriate water source in a village for a water station and housing for water purification systems. It opened in 2007 and serves 215 households of 830 people within Yangzhuang village. We charge the villagers a small fee for the water; revenue from the water sales is used to keep the operation sustainable. After the successful establishment of Yangzhuang water station, we have planned to open water stations in five other villages. And we want physically disabled people to run them.

ASIA

I have enjoyed the many countries and cultures of Asia in the last 30 years. In Thailand, I delivered wheelchairs with King Bhumibol Adulyadej and his daughter, Princess Maha Chakri Sirindhorn. In South Korea, I have been helped by Kun-Hee Lee, the chairman of Samsung, the giant electronics company. He has been generous to the Wheelchair Foundation. Chung Mong-Koo, chairman and CEO of Hyundai Motor Company and Kia Motors, has

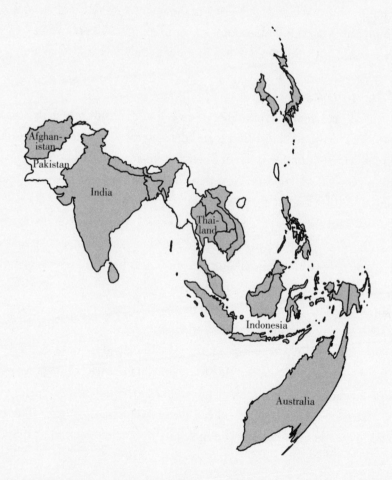

been generous as well; he surprised me with a check for more than $150,000 for the Wheelchair Foundation when I visited him at his company.

I'll also never forget a trip to Mongolia: I flew in a large Russian-made helicopter to a remote area, and on the way back, it ran out of fuel and crash-landed about a mile short of the airport! We were okay, but I could do fine without any future experiences like that one!

Of course, some of my most memorable memories of Asia come from our wheelchair distributions there. We have been fortunate to work with many wonderful organizations in the region, including the Hanoi Women's Union in Vietnam, the Red Cross in Cambodia, the Foundation for the Welfare of the Crippled in Thailand and the National Rehabilitation Center in Laos.

Philippines

A Wheelchair Foundation team went to the Philippines in 2003 and was introduced to a father and daughter. He told us that she was eight years old and had never been able to go to school because she didn't have a wheelchair. Now that we were giving her a wheelchair, she would start school immediately.

At first, she wasn't able to make the new wheelchair move and was quite distracted by all the attention she was getting as the team took pictures and talked about her. As things began to wind down and conversations turned away from her, she began to pay more attention to it. The team watched her from the other side of the room as she slowly, cautiously placed one hand and then the other on the wheels. Her face was determined as she managed to make herself move about a foot. She did this for about 10 minutes, slowly inching her way across the floor, being careful not to be noticed.

Before long, everyone realized that she had pushed herself to the opposite side of the room. The little girl stopped and acted as if nothing happened, then she looked at the group with a big smile. Later, her father said, "I have carried her since birth. She has never seen a wheelchair until today. She is a smart girl, and that is why this wheelchair is so important, so she can go to school!"

Vietnam

There are even more stories to tell about our work in Vietnam. At a distribution in Hanoi in 2003, our team met a little boy who moved himself using wooden blocks. He pulled himself along the street dragging his legs. His father brought him to our event and stood silently with the boy in the back of the room. Each time someone received a wheelchair, the boy raised himself up to watch recipients learning to use their new chairs.

When his turn finally came, the boy dragged himself to team members and carefully put his blocks on the ground. Then he lifted himself into the wheelchair under his own power. He reached down to work the brake without instruction. He looked up and, with no change in expression, placed his hands on the wheels and began to move himself around the room. He was very serious about the whole process, but our team knew he had been watching other recipients from the back of the room. He wheeled himself to his father and immediately started smiling and expressing excitement about his wheelchair. The father and the boy whispered to each other. A member of our team asked them, "Is everything okay?"

The father responded, "I am proud of my son because he has passed the test to get a wheelchair." Earlier, the boy had watched so intently because he thought that if he didn't use it correctly, he wouldn't get one. Our team asked the father what he was going to do with the wooden blocks his son used to move. He said, "Tonight my son and I will build a fire at our house and we will burn them together."

India

With more than a billion people, India is home to the world's second largest population; it also has a large population of people who need wheelchairs. The former prime minister told me that there are about 114 million people in India who are immobile.

One of our Wheelchair Foundation team members, Joel Hodge, tells the story of a family he met on a distribution in Bombay in 2002. The living conditions were horrible, the streets lined with sewage and trash. The family lived in a tin shack with dirt floors. A curtain covered an area in the back of the shack. Joel heard a lot of movement behind the curtain; he was stunned when the mother and one of her sons brought out her other son, who was held to a piece of plywood by wire. He had mild case of a neurological disease. The wires were tied loosely around his wrists and ankles. Joel was shocked. He left the shack to get a wheelchair from the van outside.

Back in the shack, Joel and his team placed the disabled son in the wheelchair. He was excited and very animated. Because of his extreme motions, Joel thought the wheelchair would do him no good. But then the young man calmed down and smiled. Joel asked family members why they kept him strapped to a board. The parents replied that he was unable to sit up unassisted but wanted to follow them whenever the family left the house. He would usually fall out of bed trying to get up; when they returned, they often found him face down in the dirt.

After Joel showed the young man how to use the wheelchair, he looked up and smiled; he understood. His sister said he was happy and that she hadn't seen him like this before. Joel wheeled him outside. The young man sat in his wheelchair, looking at everything and smiling. Joel asked his sister if he was able to sit outside very often and she said, "Never, at least not since I was a very little girl. He's always been 'my brother in the back room.' "

Not anymore.

Afghanistan

Afghanistan has suffered from armed conflict and oppressive rule for decades. Land mines and unexploded ordnance left over from previous wars and invasions kill and maim hundreds, perhaps thousands, of Afghans each year. Disease and accidents also are responsible for disability there. According to news reports, more than a million Afghan citizens are disabled, giving Afghanistan one of the highest disability rates in the world. An estimated 80,000 Afghans have lost limbs, mainly as a result of land mines.

A team sponsored by Rotarians traveled to Kabul in June 2003 to deliver 240 wheelchairs. One of the recipients was a 19-year-old boy named Najib. He had been confined to his bed for 18 months because of an accident. The day after he received his wheelchair, one of our volunteers looked out of his office window: "We noticed a large crowd outside. Najib was the center of attention; he was the hero. He was proudly briefing children on the operation of his new wheelchair. He was surrounded by dozens of curious children asking him how he felt and touching his wheelchair. He said, 'I do not want to go home. I want to go to the shop down the street, and school, and play outside, to feel the outside air.' "

I went to Kabul in September 2003 to distribute the first of 5,000 wheelchairs delivered in partnership with the U.S. Department of State, the Department of Defense, our friends at LDS Charities and the Knights of Columbus. For several years, the State Department provided funds to us to sponsor wheelchairs, and the Defense Department provided transportation of wheelchair containers to countries with land mines and civil unrest. We were met at our plane by five U.S. armored vehicles with machine guns on their roofs. The sight made us all very aware that we were in a war zone. The soldiers escorted us to an armed compound outside Kabul that was to be our home while we were in the country. U.S. military officers advised us that for security reasons, we could distribute wheelchairs only in the compound.

On the day of the distribution, the first buses began to arrive at 9:30 a.m. Officials from the State Department and the U.S. Agency for International Development had measured most of the recipients for their new wheelchairs a few days earlier, so they already had some idea of what was coming. Family members and U.S. soldiers assisted the recipients as they made their way off the buses. Many were carried, some crawled and some used simple handmade crutches. Everyone took a seat under an awning and each recipient patiently waited his or her turn to receive a brand new, shiny red wheelchair. One of the first recipients was a young man who excitedly wanted to show his new wheelchair agility to the other recipients; he spun around in his chair, pushed himself in circles and "popped wheelies." Another young man crawled over to his wheelchair but was unable to get into it by himself—the lower half of his body was missing as a result of a land mine explosion. A group of soldiers rushed to his side and lifted him into his wheelchair.

As soon as everyone was seated, we photographed each recipient. With few exceptions, everyone seemed much older than his or her actual age. It's no surprise—at the time, the average life expectancy in Afghanistan was just 47 years. Life there is difficult.

As the distribution came to a close, we noticed a man dragging himself along the ground with his hands. A land mine had blown away his entire lower body. His only protection from the rocks and dirt was a piece of cardboard he had tied around the bottom of his torso. He told us he had missed the bus, but hoped there was an extra wheelchair for him. He had a wife and six children; he wanted the wheelchair so he could go back to work and provide for his family. Several soldiers quickly brought him one, and as they picked him up and put him in it, he placed his right hand over his heart and smiled. This was his way of thanking us not only for his new wheelchair—but also for his new way of life.

Throughout the event, I saw many American soldiers moved to tears. They thanked us and the representatives from LDS Charities and the Knights of Columbus (which has supported us in other countries as well) for our generosity and compassion for immobile Afghans. The soldiers were grateful for the opportunity to participate in an event that made such a difference to people and spread the joy of unselfish giving.

EASTERN EUROPE

I have enjoyed visiting Eastern Europe frequently over the years. My ancestors came from there. I had the pleasure of holding wheelchair distributions there with Gen. Joe Ralston (USAF-Ret.) in 2001

and 2002, when he was the commander of NATO, the North Atlantic Treaty Organization. One of his responsibilities was humanitarian assistance in the region. On wheelchair deliveries, we met with the leaders of Latvia, Estonia, Romania, the Czech Republic, Bosnia-Herzegovina and Hungary. I learned about the new friendships we were forming with these former Soviet satellite countries. As my first wheelchair delivery was in Eastern Europe (Romania), I have returned there many times to help the physically disabled. Here are some of their stories.

Bosnia-Herzegovina

While we were in the former Yugoslavia, we met a Bosnian man who began to cry when he told us of his teenage son, who was very large. He told us that when they were walking down a road one day, the son stepped on a cluster bomb. It blew him up into the air, and he landed on another cluster bomb, which also blew up. Then he landed on a third bomb.

"By the time I got to him, he was covered with blood," the man said. "I was sure my son was dead." The man got his son to a first-aid station. The staff there said the station did not have any blood to help him. Drivers took him to a hospital that had a supply of blood. The man said that as they were going to the hospital, he could feel the life draining out of his son. "But we got to the hospital and God was with us," the man said. His son was treated and lived. He was released from the hospital 11 months later. He had lost both legs at his hips and one arm. He had lost his sight in one eye. He had lost his hearing in one ear. But he was alive.

The father said the only thing his son wanted to be able to do was to sit in the sun, but he was too heavy to carry. A wheelchair would let him do that. We gave his son one. That day, I realized how much a simple thing like sitting in the sun could mean to a human being. Every person should at least have the right to do that.

Turkey

I had the opportunity to meet with His All Holiness Ecumenical Patriarch Bartholomew, the spiritual leader of the Greek Orthodox Church, on three occasions. At a distribution in Istanbul (known to the Greeks as Constantinople), we delivered wheelchairs at church headquarters and at a rehabilitation center outside of the city. I enjoyed learning about the Greek Orthodox faith, as I enjoy learning about other world religions. I also joined His Holiness on a trip to Cuba for the dedication of the first church built there since Fidel Castro came to power. In Cuba, we held wheelchair distributions and enjoyed having dinner two nights in a row with the patriarch, Castro and the former king and queen of Greece.

MIDDLE EAST

We have been delivering wheelchairs in this vital region of the world since 2000. We have sent many to Israel, and we brought wheelchairs to the Palestinian Territories, Egypt, Iran, Iraq, Jordan, Syria, Lebanon and other destinations. Many wheelchairs brought to the region are labeled with a patch that reads, "Given in Friendship from the People of the United States." For several years, under a Middle East Initiative, we partnered with the U.S. Department of State and the Department of Defense on this important mission.

Jordan

Seeking to bring relief and hope to physically disabled citizens in Amman, the Wheelchair Foundation teamed up with the Al-Hussein Society to deliver 240 wheelchairs in 2001. The wheelchairs went to a rehabilitation center for the physically challenged established by the late King Hussein and Queen Noor. The center serves many young children. One of the recipients, a young boy, grinned

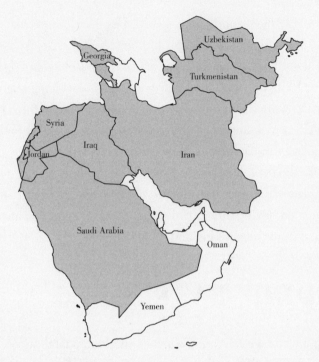

from ear to ear as he talked about how much he liked his "bicycle." Though not a bike in any traditional sense, the boy's new wheelchair did give him the ability to get outside, to race with other boys, to go exploring and to go to school. The "Seventh Circle Man," a 40-year-old who for years had to crawl around the Seventh Circle, a busy Amman intersection, received a wheelchair. Family and friends no longer had to worry about him being run over because he had to crawl in traffic. Other recipients included a 20-year-old man with no use of his arms and with only one leg who painted a picture with his toes of the two Americans who presented him a wheelchair.

"I am very thankful for the Wheelchair Foundation because of the opportunities given to children," said Jordanian Princess Majda Raad, who runs the Al-Hussein Society. "The gift of a new wheelchair gives our children the gift of a new perspective and lets them experience and explore their environment." The wheelchair deliveries in Amman were made possible by the Rotary Club of Woodside/ Portola Valley, California.

We went back to Jordan twice in 2004. As part of one trip, we returned to Amman to give more wheelchairs to the rehabilitation center. We were met at the airport by a delegation of Jordanian Rotarians, who have been very committed to getting wheelchairs distributed throughout the country. I had been to the center so many times that the children there know me now. Queen Rania joined us at one distribution.

LATIN AND SOUTH AMERICA

We discovered an overwhelming need for wheelchairs in Mexico, Central and South America and the islands of the Caribbean. Here are some of the stories from our distributions there.

The Bahamas

In 2000, I called a good friend in Florida, Jack Drury, and recruited him to help me launch the Wheelchair Foundation. He had just turned 70, was winding down his career as a public relations consultant, looking forward to semi-retirement and more golf in Fort Lauderdale, Florida. I had been one of his clients. He agreed to open an office for us in Florida. One of his first assignments was to go on a distribution of wheelchairs in Nassau, the Bahamas, which was a place he always knew as a resort. He went to the building wheredisabled children were kept for the day while their parents worked. They had no wheelchairs and were playing on the ground.

"When I picked up the first boy and put him in his own wheel-

chair, I was filled with joy knowing I was doing something meaning-ful—not worrying whether a little golf ball went in to a hole," Jack said. "I know that my work all these years has made a difference."

Bolivia

In 2002, we delivered wheelchairs in Bolivia with our partners at LDS Charities. Were it not for a nun who made it her life's work to rescue severely disabled orphans, two of the children who received wheelchairs that day might never have made it. One had been aban-doned near death when she was just a few days old. The other, an eight-year-old boy, lost his mother during childbirth and was aban-doned by his alcoholic father just one week prior to the distribution. The nun and her orphanage took the children in.

With their new wheelchairs, the children received some independence and the ability to go where they wanted. They once had been left lying in the street; now they could move about and see things that were once out of their reach. Mobility for them and other physically disabled orphans was also an answer to the sister's prayers. Because the children with wheelchairs could now interact freely among themselves, she could spend more time with others who needed help.

Peru

In 2012, my son, David, led a dozen of his classmates from his alma mater, Princeton University, on yet another wheelchair mission, this time to Peru. David is the president of the Wheelchair Foundation. Members of Princeton's Class of '77 raised the funding for and distributed wheelchairs in Guatemala (2002, 2007) and Vietnam (2002). David's classmate, Henry Posner III, helped make Peru a good choice for the group—Henry's company, Railroad Development Corp., is a major shareholder in the train company there and it helped deliver 500 wheelchairs and class volunteers to distribution sites. For its weeklong visit for its 35th reunion year, the group raised $95,000. To deliver them, the group traveled through and over more than 50 tunnels and 50 bridges by rail to places as high as 16,000 feet!

In remarks at each of the distributions, Henry made a powerful statement: "Movement and motion are basic human rights."

At one distribution, classmate Bill Farrell met a 13-year-old girl who had just received her chair. Her hands were contorted and her gaze cocked to one side. She was struggling to hold on to a bright pink box containing a Barbie-like doll. The girl did not respond to requests to look up for her picture. Bill addressed the elderly woman at her side. After exchanging greetings and names, he asked, "Is this your daughter?" "My granddaughter." The woman looked weary and Bill was not sure of her age.

"How will this chair change your granddaughter's life?" he asked. The woman began to weep. As the tears reached her jaw line, she wiped them with the back of a weathered, calloused hand and said, "Please excuse me." Bill could tell she felt ashamed for crying in front of him. "It's alright," he said, hugging her. "I can tell your tears are tears of relief."

"Relief," she repeated. "Relief and gratitude. My granddaughter is 13 years old. Her mother has to work. There is no father. I care for the three children. I've been carrying my granddaughter for 13 years. I can no longer carry her." She paused and sighed. "She is too big and I am too old. Thank you. Thank you, so much." As they hugged again, Bill felt the sting of tears in his own eyes.

"Gracias. Gracias," she said patting his shoulders.

"You are most welcome," Bill said. "It is our great honor to give your granddaughter the gift of mobility."

"You have given ME the gift," said the old woman as she left, pushing her granddaughter with great ease.

Brazil

In 2000, I received a call from Queen Sofia of Spain, who asked me to deliver some wheelchairs to Brazil. She and King Juan Carlos were going to visit then-President Cardosa and First Lady Ruth Correa Leite to celebrate Spain's great relationship with Brazil. I said I would be happy to come and asked when she wanted me. She said on Monday; it was already Thursday. I said I couldn't make the trip on such short notice but that I would air-express some wheelchairs. She said that was not what she wanted. She asked me to attend a distribution in Brazil in person. She said she would call back in two hours so I could give her my travel arrangements. I quickly learned that a queen is used to getting her way!

After my team scrambled to get visas and prepare a flight plan, I packed my plane with wheelchairs and took off for Brazil. We arranged to have a distribution at the Spanish embassy in the capital city, Brasilia. The king, queen, president and first lady helped with the delivery while a thousand VIP guests in formal attire waited two hours for the celebration to begin. I spoke with the Spanish ambassador, who had arranged and organized the ceremony. He said the event was the most difficult in his career. But at least 40 wheelchair recipients were happy—they each had a chance to meet the king and queen and their president and first lady.

On a Sunday afternoon in the capital, Wheelchair Foundation team members stopped at a local church and asked the priest if he knew of any people in the area who needed a wheelchair but could not afford one. He said he did, got into a car and led us into the countryside down red sandy roads. Team members arrived at a small cinderblock and tin shack. They were introduced to a family of eight. The family's "farm" had chickens and ducks in the yard, a single old swayback horse and a small garden. It had an open well with a bucket and rope for bringing up water. There wasn't much else. Team members were led into a single-room house, with one bed and some mats on the floor. In one corner was a large chair filled with rags. In it sat a girl with arms and legs as thin as fragile twigs. She had beautiful brown eyes and a very nice smile but couldn't speak. Her mother told the team that she was 18 years old and had been like this since birth. She lived in the chair and was unable to care for herself.

The team put her in a wheelchair and adjusted the leg rests to accommodate her withered limbs. Soon her sisters began wheeling her around the yard. The girls laughed and smiled. They told team members that they liked the wheelchair because it meant that they wouldn't have to carry their sister everywhere anymore. They were also excited because they could take her to more places with them. Her father, who had been talking with the priest, knelt down with him and they prayed. When they finished the prayer, the father came and thanked the team.

"Today is my birthday," he said. "This very morning I got up and asked God for one gift for my birthday, for someone to help my daughter. This Sunday, God sent you to me for my birthday. I thanked the Lord and I thank you."

Mexico

Second to China, we have delivered more wheelchairs in Mexico than in any other country—more than 150,000. Mexico's shared border with the U.S. makes deliveries there easier to attend for Rotary Clubs sponsoring hands-on service projects.

I joined Rotarians from northern California to deliver 240 wheelchairs at a small soccer stadium in Texcoco, outside of Mexico City, in 2001. The population of the city and its surrounding area is more than 25 million people. It is estimated that 1.2 million Mexicans need a wheelchair but cannot afford one.

One of them was Martina Miranda, age 42, who had been physically disabled by polio. She told our Rotary friends that she'd had a wheelchair about 20 years earlier. It lasted only five years and she could not afford another one. To get to the bus each morning, her nephew wheeled her on a hand truck as she sat on a milk crate. She worked at a roadside stand selling shoe polish. Other times, she walked on her knees. Her 85-year-old mother had lifted and helped her for the past 42 years. They had tears of joy in their eyes when they received her wheelchair. Martina said, "I have prayed so long for another wheelchair, and I knew that my prayers would be answered." Her mother said that they could never have afforded such a beautiful wheelchair and that the gift would make the remaining years of her life much easier.

Rotarian Jon Grant has been an ambassador between Rotarians worldwide and the Foundation, along with his wife, Linda; they do important work in Mexico, especially with young people from the

U.S. In recent distributions there, he has taken high school students from California with him.

"They come from comfortable lives in the U.S., not realizing that not everyone in the world has cell phones and computers and TVs," Jon said. "They get to help somebody less fortunate and they realize that one person can really make a difference. They learn that by working together, their efforts are changing people's lives."

Rotarians from RC Hemosillo del Desierto have been some of our strongest partners in Mexico through the years. Jorge Ibarra, a lawyer from the club, cannot forget an old man in a coastal town who made a living out of collecting and recycling aluminum cans. Before getting one of our wheelchairs, he moved from place to place in an old wheelchair tied together with rusty wire at the seat and back levels. When Jorge's team helped man into the new chair, members noticed cuts, scars and even infected wounds on his back and buttocks.

"This delivery is one of the most life-changing experiences I have ever had," Jorge says.

One of my most memorable distribution stories involves a woman named Maria, who worked for my family for more than a decade. When she heard that we were going to Mexico City, she told me she had a nephew there, Angel, who had lost his eyesight and mobility because of a terminal disease. She asked if we could give him a wheelchair so that he could be mobile during the time he had left. I said, "Of course," and asked her to arrange getting him to our distribution.

His parents found us the day of the event. Through tears of gratitude they said Angel had received his wheelchair and wanted to thank me. They brought him to me and I took his hands and spoke to him so he would know where I was. Then he grasped my hands, turned his blind eyes toward my eyes and said, "I will see you in heaven." He touched me so deeply that I was not able to answer him.

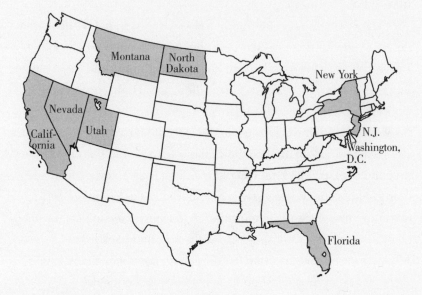

UNITED STATES

We have not limited our work to countries outside of the U.S. We have Wheelchair Foundation offices in California, Florida and Las Vegas. To date, we have donated more than 33,000 wheelchairs to physically disabled people in America.

We began delivering wheelchairs across the U.S. with the Salvation Army in 2000 and distributed wheelchairs to senior citizens at the Crow Indian Nation in Montana. The Oakland A's baseball organization and one of its owners, my friend Ken Hofmann, and other sponsors provided wheelchairs to people in Oakland, California. Rotarians and Major League Baseball sponsored wheelchairs in New York and New Jersey that were distributed by Goodwill Industries and Catholic Charities. The late builder Ralph Englestad and his wife, Betty, agreed to sponsor wheelchairs for needy people in North

Dakota and Nevada. With several sponsors, we joined former Utah governor Mike Leavitt to reduce immobility in his state.

In 2004, we launched several new programs in the U.S. We began giving sports wheelchairs to local organizations throughout the country in association with the U.S. Paralympics. The International Association of Firefighters (IAFF) helped us deliver basic mobility wheelchairs to local communities and agreed to help us expand the delivery of sports wheelchairs. At an event in Concord, California, in 2004, the Foundation and the firefighters joined representatives of Wells Fargo Bank and Catholic Charities of the East Bay to distribute wheelchairs. Wells Fargo Bank of Rossmoor donated funds to provide wheelchairs in Contra Costa County, 30 of which were distributed at the Concord ceremony. Catholic Charities identified the recipients and hosted the event.

In 2004, we also delivered wheelchairs to Walter Reed Army Medical Center in Washington, DC. The wheelchairs went mainly to help amputees returning from the war in Iraq. While we were making arrangements to deliver the regular wheelchairs, we found out that there was a gymnasium that patients were encouraged to use. We delivered 10 sports wheelchairs to the gym for wheelchair basketball games. Nationally, our sponsors have donated wheelchairs to veterans and supporting organizations.

Of course many of our terrific partners, donors and volunteers come from the U.S. Their stories are uplifting, too.

Inspired by Miguel Tejada, the former Oakland A's shortstop known for his grand slams, Justin Gonsalves, 17, made a grand slam of his own in 2002. Justin, a Boy Scout, was a senior at Logan High School in Union City, California, when he attended an A's game and saw video footage of the team distributing wheelchairs in the Dominican Republic with the Wheelchair Foundation. He immediately decided to do something for the physically disabled as his Eagle Scout project.

After meeting with his troop leader, he planned a pancake breakfast fundraiser and a direct mail and outreach campaign to his community. One of the key requirements for his community service badge was to complete a minimum of 100 hours of community work. Justin could receive credit for each hour worked individually, as well as each hour of community service given by friends and family. He pulled together a team and logged more than 130 hours of service while raising $8,328.49 for the Foundation.

"It feels good to be a Boy Scout and help disabled people like this," Justin said. "It makes me even prouder to be a Scout." Justin's donation enabled the Foundation to deliver 111 wheelchairs to physically disabled people in Mexico. He participated in the distribution, changing many lives—including his own, and in the process learned more about how to be a leader.

We all could learn something from one of our most devoted donors and volunteers, Dr. Scharleen Colant, who passed away in 2010. A globetrotter like me, Scharleen first called the Wheelchair Foundation in 2006 to become a donor and volunteer at age 85. She learned of our work as a member of the Rotary Club of San Francisco and wanted to get involved. She gave away hundreds of wheelchairs on trips to Vietnam, Cambodia, Thailand and Chile—and right here at home, in Astoria, Queens, New York.

She went to Astoria because of the "Miracle On the Hudson"— that amazing winter day in January 2009 when U.S. Airways Captain Chesley "Sully" Sullenberger safely landed a plane loaded with 155 passengers and crew in the Hudson River. Scharleen's husband Ernest had been an airline pilot; she knew how hard flying an airplane is. Moved by Captain Sullenberger's courage and competence, she called us the very next day to donate a container of wheelchairs for low-income people in New York in Sully's honor. At an event at Goodwill Industries, she met with each recipient personally. She also got to meet Captain Sullenberger later at a Foundation fundraising dinner in our headquarters in Danville, California—which is also the captain's hometown.

"Everybody should have the opportunity to sponsor a wheelchair and give it to someone along the way in their life travels," Scharleen said. "They have no idea what they're missing. I would go around the world to give a wheelchair to someone if I knew it would help them. This experience has given me something in my life that I never expected."

Sully Sullenberger and Scharleen Colant—heroes and leaders both.

• • •

Since we launched the Wheelchair Foundation, we have given away nearly a million wheelchairs in more than 150 countries. Behind every one of them is a story like the ones you have just read. Yet we have a lot of work left to do. The World Health Organization estimates that more than 25 million people around the globe are immobile. But based on our firsthand experience, we believe the number is actually 3 percent of the world's population, or about 200 million people. Giving all of them wheelchairs will be a huge undertaking and will cost billions of dollars.

But I feel there is no choice. In most cases, we are helping people who have no dignity, no hope, no future. Then suddenly, with the gift of a wheelchair, they feel as though they have become part of the human race. They now have pride and they now have hope. They may not be able to do everything they want, but at least they will be able to be more independent, to open a milk bar, go back to school, splash in a fountain or just sit in the sun.

And sometimes getting a wheelchair helps create leaders among recipients, volunteers and donors—just look at Josh Routh, Justin Gonsalves, Xie Yanhong and Hainan Yin.

"The work we do with the Wheelchair Foundation has helped Josh evolve from a contributing member of his community to truly being a leader in the community," says his dad, Don. "Josh has a strong sense of pride about how we have helped so many people in so many different countries. He has also developed strong communication skills and is able to grab a microphone and speak through an interpreter to hundreds of people."

We cannot forget how much the gift of a wheelchair can also help family members and caregivers: parents who no longer have to carry a child everywhere, siblings who no longer have to pick up a heavy brother or sister. In many cases, a wheelchair gives them freedom, too—freedom to get a job or education, to get out of the house more, to live a fuller life.

But we need your help. Every wheelchair changes a life. What a simple way to give purpose to your life.

I started with major museums at the Smithsonian Institution in Washington, D.C. Pat and I celebrated "The American Presidency" exhibit at the National Museum of American History in 2000. In 2004, below, the museum opened "The Price of Freedom." Retired General Colin Powell, at right, attended the grand opening. His uniform is on display in the exhibit.

We also supported the renovation of the Mammal Hall at the National Museum of Natural History. Kids love seeing the tiger, frozen by taxidermists as it leaps on its prey.

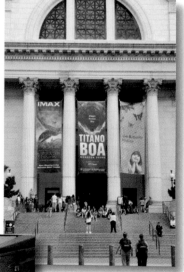

(Courtesy Smithsonian Institution)

This is the Huey helicopter from Vietnam that the curators at the National Museum of American History included in "The Price of Freedom."

My support for the Smithsonian opened doors to museums in China. These are officials with the Beijing Museum of Natural History.

This is their museum, but Beijing is planning to build a new one.

Does this Beijing display look real enough for you? It's an example of "bringing museums to life" that I am talking about.

The Museum of Natural History in Dalian was the first museum in China to which we donated mounted animal specimens.

Dalian officials pulled out the stops in 2006 to show me what they could do with my specimens starting with this magnificent bull elephant.

Then we got down to signing more agreements.

The Shanghai Science and Technology Museum received our first donation—my spider collection!

Shanghai museum curators have helped me launch my vision in China in "bringing museums to life."

Here is the illustration of the new Shanghai Museum of Natural History (branch of SSTM). It will include a large space for my specimen donations. (Courtesy SSTM)

My good friend Madam Zuo Huanchen is the Board Chairman of both the Shanghai Science and Technology Museum and Shanghai Science Education Development Foundation.

Madam Zuo and I met my young friend Kun Sha in the Spider Hall.

I signed an agreement with Shanghai museum officials in 2010. I made a few remarks at the event about the importance of teaching natural history.

I joined Madam Zuo and other officials on stage to celebrate the grand opening of the Animals World exhibit in the SSTM.

Former Shanghai Mayor Han Zheng, now a Party secretary, has been a strong supporter of my museum and wheelchair work.

Shanghai museum officials have kindly acknowledged my contributions with this biographical display.

Here is the current Tianjin Museum of Natural History.

This was the signing ceremony for my donation of animal specimens to the Tianjin Museum of Natural History in 2011.

Tianjin has built a new natural history museum.

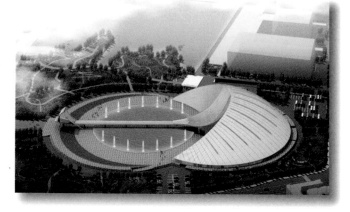

The Shandong Museum has big plans for our animal specimens.

The lobby of the Shandong Museum features this spectacular dome.

Shandong Museum designers have come up with this unique idea—a "tree house" inside the museum that would provide views of the different nature exhibits in the hall. (Courtesy Shandong Museum)

The tree house would include a biographical exhibit of my life and help spread my message to young people in China.

I've continued my meetings with top officials in Shandong.

The Yangzhou Museum's "Window of World Animals" exhibit is a theme park integrated with ecological environments, scientific education, amusement and recreation.

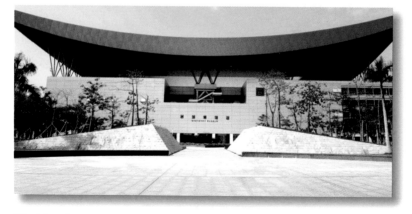

The Shenzhen Museum houses my specimens now, but the city is planning to build a stand-alone natural history museum.

The new Chongqing Museum of Natural History, shown in this architect's rendering, is another newer partner in nature exhibits and natural history education.

I signed an agreement with the Chongqing Museum in 2012.

Some museum officials have called me a "rock star," but I am content to sign a few autographs for fans of natural history and museums.

Here is my bust in the Chongqing Museum. I appreciate the recognition my Chinese museum and education partners give me.

And the Chinese also want to recognize the work of the Wheelchair Foundation. This statue was created for the new Shanghai Museum of Natural History.

Some National History Day finalists wanted to see my bust at the National Museum of American History at the Smithsonian.

We are looking forward to working with the Hubei Provincial Museum, which offers new and exciting prospects for growth.

The museum at Qingdao Binhai University is an important partner for us because of the opportunity to reach thousands of college students and teachers for natural history education.

I signed a memorandum of understanding with Qingdao Binhai University in 2012 to continue to work together.

Qingdao Binhai University made me its honorary president for my donations to its museum. I have received many honorary titles in China over the years.

In Beijing, the National Zoological Museum, along with China's Institute of Zoology and Academy of Sciences, are promising potential partners in research and education.

We think China's zoologists and nature scientists could help us significantly improve natural history education in their country.

Our taxidermists have created a specimen of a prehistoric cave bear. Compare it to the grizzly bear to the left. We plan to place one in as many museums as we can.

We want to exhibit the cave bear side by side with polar bears in museums to give kids a good idea of just how awesome cave bears were.

My team and I continue to review museum plans and proposals.

We continue to try to bring museums to life with specimens like this bull elephant.

As I have said for years, all I want in return for a gift is a smile!

Chapter 10
CATHEDRALS OF LEARNING

A museum is not a first-hand contact:
It is an illustrated lecture.
And what one wants is the actual vital touch.

D.H. Lawrence

I want to reinvent museums.

I don't want them just to put objects on display, to be big boxy warehouses of things and echoes. I want museums to bring objects to life—and in the process, help educate and develop new leaders.

Let me give you an example of what I mean.

As you read a few chapters ago, one of my passions is big game hunting. I have a large collection of mounted animals—lions, water buffalo, bear and more. I have donated many of these specimens to museums. At some museums, the curators have "parked" them one after another behind glass, collecting dust.

But at the Animals World exhibit at the Shanghai Science and Technology Museum in China, an African lioness leaps from a rock toward a warthog she plans to kill for food for her cubs. A leopard sits on a tree branch with his kill for the day, a springbok gazelle.

Nearby, a hyena holds a half-eaten antelope in its jaws as a vulture tries to move in on the hyena's meal. You can hear the trumpet call of a bull elephant in the background, along with the roar of a tiger and other animal voices.

Very few people ever get to see or hear these activities and sounds in their actual natural setting in the wild. People would not see them in a zoo, either—zoo animals spend most of their lives in captivity doing little more than waiting to be fed under the gaze of tourists, if the city is lucky enough to even have a zoo. At best, a nature filmmaker's camera will produce two-dimensional images of scenes at a distance. And what about animals that are extinct or near extinction? No, only in this exhibit, and the few others like it in the world, would an interested child or parent have the opportunity to see a lioness like this one frozen in a moment in time, a point of important animal behavior.   It is not just some stuffed animal gathering dust behind glass—it's as close to that real-life moment of a predator and its prey as pretty much anyone will ever get.

And it works. It has an impact. It helps teach children and adults about the real world.

"It is so realistic!" says Shen Xuan, 7, a first-grade student from a city near Shanghai. He was looking at the hyena with the antelope. That's the reaction I want. For Africa is not a zoo where people control, feed and lock up creatures in a pen. The wilds of Africa are about "survival of the fittest" and the continuing cycle of life, and that includes the food chain and death. And to be successful in their own lives—to be better students, citizens and potential leaders of the future—they need to learn about this.

Xuan was one of hundreds of children in the museum's animal exhibit that day in 2012. Like so many of the other kids, he was visiting for the first time and was there with his family. His father, Young, said Xuan had only seen wild animals on TV and brought Xuan to the museum because he wanted him to study the specimens up close and "see them for real." Young was himself a teacher—high school physics—and appreciated having a place to take Xuan so that he can get to know nature and the animal world better. He wanted his son to be a better student and he feels getting him out of a book, away from a TV and into the animal hall will help.

As you may have guessed by now, I sponsored the Animals World exhibit. The Shanghai Science and Technology Museum is one of more than a dozen museums that I am involved with in China, where I see enormous opportunity to help improve learning and to use museums as platforms in a larger plan to help educate, inspire and develop future generations of public and private sector leaders around the world.

My interest in museums began with my passion for cars—given what was to come in my life, it's appropriate that it started with wheels. I started with my plans for the Blackhawk Country Club. I wanted to make it prestigious, one of the finest in the U.S. My team hired chefs, captains and waiters from Miami's best hotels and designed exclusive rooms for private dining. After it opened in 1980, it was featured on *Lifestyles of the Rich and Famous* as one of the best clubs in the nation. As part of the benefits, I thought a Rolls-Royce limousine would be attractive for use for weddings and important events at the club.

I heard about a Rolls-Royce Silver Wraith for sale by a classic car dealer in Arizona. When I flew to look at it, I bought it. But the transmission needed work. A lot of work. Two months later, when it still wasn't fixed, I went back to the dealer. Like any unsatisfied customer, I asked for my money back. But the salesman assured me it would be fixed. I trusted him. I ended up buying three more cars from him: a 1937 Cord Sportsman, a 1939 Lincoln convertible coupe, and a 1928 Cadillac Dual-Cowl Phaeton convertible. He convinced me they were good buys. For once, I'd met a better salesperson! He ignited my interest in classic cars and I was hooked.

He impressed me so much that after I returned home, I thought that I should hire this salesman and start a classic auto collection.

That salesman was Don Williams. He was enthusiastic about the chance to put together a group of the some of the finest classic cars in the world. After I hired him, we heard about an incredible set of 13 cars for sale in England. The first time we became aware of it we knew it was the greatest collection on the market at that time. We traveled to Europe and negotiated a multimillion-dollar deal for it. The purchase needed to close immediately. Otherwise, a bank was going to take possession of the cars and their price would double. I called a friend at a bank and explained the situation. I asked him to wire me the money. We'd take care of the details later. Luckily, he agreed. With that, we owned an impressive collection of some of the world's great classic cars. We were still used car dealers at heart, and classic automobiles are the most desirable used cars.

It was the start of a global buying spree in search of the world's greatest cars. Our fleet grew with new purchases and trades. Sometimes we'd even buy a collection of 100 cars just to get the three or four gems. The history, beautiful craftsmanship and artistry of these classics thrilled me. But their purchase, storage and maintenance were expensive. Then it occurred to me: the cars were impressive as pieces of artwork. They deserved to be shared with the public in a classic auto museum. I started working on plans to establish one. That way, people from all over the world would be able to enjoy them.

I approached several universities as possible partners. At the University of California, Berkeley, I met Michael Heyman, the chancellor. He was intrigued by the idea of an automotive museum. Under my proposal, the university would eventually own the museum and many donated cars. That excited him. We agreed to an arrangement. One part of the museum would house antique cars; the other part would exhibit some of Berkeley's treasures in anthropology and paleontology, an important area of study for children.

Always the developer, I had the museum constructed as part of a shopping center at Blackhawk. I hoped it would draw people to shop when they came to see the cars. The museum opened its doors to the public in 1988. The building turned out to be striking and showed off the cars as the masterpieces they are—"rolling works of art." The collection was worth $100 million. To help get kids to the museum, we started the Children's Education and Transportation Fund, which helps pay field trip expenses for museum visits by public, private and parochial schools in Contra Costa County.

Today, the Blackhawk Museum is recognized around the world. It currently displays more than 90 classic cars, many of which are one-of-a-kind and date from around the turn of the century. Some of them are on loan to us from friends who own some of the finest private collections in the world. Some of these cars would never be seen by the public were it not for the museum. The display evolves and changes constantly. Over the years, the museum has housed Clark Gable's 1935 Duisenberg roadster, Franklin Roosevelt's 1938 Packard Phaeton, Rita Hayworth's 1953 Cadillac coupe (one of two in the world) and Queen Elizabeth's 1954 Daimler limousine, among others of note. Blackhawk has the most dramatic presentation of coach-built cars in the world without exception. This unique collection ensures that significant automotive treasures that blend art, technology, culture and history will be exhibited for public enjoyment as well as educational enrichment for years to come.

Twelve years after we opened the museum, UC Berkeley decided it was too far from its campus and withdrew some of its educational support. So with the university out of the picture, we expanded the educational focus of the museum with a number of rotating displays, including one of the world's great collections of automotive art. In 1999, my son David headed the museum for four years and initiated and expanded its role as an affiliate of the Smithsonian Institution.

Numerous world-class Smithsonian traveling exhibitions were brought out and displayed to the public during this period. Later, we replaced them with a wheelchair gallery—an educational multimedia exhibit about the history of the wheelchair and the mission of the Wheelchair Foundation.

The positive feedback we received from the Blackhawk Museum and its exhibits, especially the wheelchair gallery, taught me I might be on to something. Here is a sample of the comments from our visitors' book people can write in when they leave:

"Amazing car museum and amazing what other gift is given to those in need of wheelchairs. God bless you ten-fold!"

"We found the auto exhibits to be outstanding, but the wheelchair room was incredibly moving. Such wonderful work to be doing!"

"As a fabricator of automobile parts, I've always wanted to visit the Blackhawk Museum. As a polio survivor, I doubly admire this man, Ken Behring. Your generosity brings happy thoughts!"

Wow. I was learning that museums can have an impact. A big one. I wanted to do more. My enthusiasm for big game hunting gave me the opportunity. My financial success allowed me to travel to one of the most amazing places in the world—Africa. I was captivated by its undeveloped beauty and excited by the challenge of hunting some of the most powerful creatures on earth. Although I know many people do not approve of hunting, I've always been intrigued by the skill and determination required for the sport.

I started hunting as a kid in Wisconsin. Today, I hunt in what I consider to be a responsible manner, respecting all legal quotas and paying required charges. The fees I pay help fund conservation research, operations of schools and hospitals and poaching prevention in tribal lands. I belong to Safari Club International (SCI), an organization that promotes hunting but also funds research and conservation initiatives. SCI's 55,000 members include the late General

Norman Schwarzkopf, former President George H.W. Bush—an honorary lifetime member—and other notable people.

After years hunting in Africa and other parts of the world, I had a large collection of mounted animals. I felt the specimens would be ideal for museum or educational purposes. I contacted several natural history museums to see if they needed any new animal displays. I went first to the American Museum of Natural History in New York. Although it was interested, it didn't need more specimens. By chance, I thought of Mike Heyman from Berkeley, who was now the secretary of the Smithsonian Institution in Washington, DC. When I called him in 1997 to ask if he knew of a museum that might be interested in my collection, he said, "You have found one. How soon can you be here?"

I flew to Washington. We toured the Smithsonian's collection and looked at the specimens, many donated by Teddy Roosevelt. A number of them had seen better days. Mike explained to me that not only did many of the current specimens need repair, but also the science and educational exhibits desperately needed to be updated. Excited by the idea of sharing my enjoyment of animals, I decided to donate $20 million and the best of my collection of mounted animals and animal skins to the Smithsonian. This money helped the Smithsonian build the finest mammal hall in the world. It includes impressive dioramas that explain how mammals have evolved and adapted to habitat changes over millions of years. It took three years to complete the 25,000-square-foot gallery—triple the space of the old one.

The Kenneth E. Behring Family Hall of Mammals opened in the fall of 2003. It displays a wide variety of creatures, from rainforest to desert dwellers, from the Australian koala to the American bison. Not only is the scope impressive but the presentation is unique— enhanced by creative multimedia systems. One display lets visitors feel how cold it is for an Arctic squirrel as it hibernates in its burrow at 34 degrees below zero. Displays of African watering holes are enhanced with the sounds of rainstorms. The hall houses 274 specimens in all, including such greats as a leopard, a lion, a walrus and a brown bear. Teddy Roosevelt's prized white rhinoceros is there, too. It is a "Mammal Family Reunion." I'm proud to have my name associated with it. It has set a standard for the other exhibitions of the Smithsonian, as well as for museums around the world.

I suppose the Smithsonian knew a good thing when it saw one, because it continued to court me. After Mike Heyman resigned, Lawrence Small became the secretary of the Smithsonian in 2000. He asked about my other museum interests. Looking back on my roots in the poverty of the Depression, I knew that I'd come a long way from the boy who owned a single pair of overalls. I also knew that I owed a debt of gratitude to the country that had allowed me to achieve my dreams. I was inspired to show the history, opportunity and future that can be attained with the freedom we have in America. The Smithsonian wanted to revamp the National Museum of American History (NMAH). It sounded like a fit. I agreed to donate $80 million to modernize the museum's exhibits and to showcase the American Dream in the nation's history. I can think of no better way to repay my country than to pay tribute to the people who made it, and continue to make it, the greatest country in the world.

My two gifts, totaling $100 million, amounted to the largest charitable contribution in the Smithsonian's history. In recognition of the second gift, the building that houses the National Museum of American History was designated as the "Kenneth E. Behring Center."

One of the first exhibits to result from my NMAH donation was "The American Presidency: A Glorious Burden." It opened in 2000 with 11 sections set in more than 9,000 square feet of gallery space. Its 900-plus treasures include one of George Washington's military uniforms; the portable lap desk that Thomas Jefferson designed and on which he wrote the Declaration of Independence; the top hat

Abraham Lincoln wore the night he was assassinated; Franklin Roosevelt's pince-nez glasses—even Warren G. Harding's silk pajamas and Bill Clinton's saxophone!

In November 2004, the Smithsonian opened the next exhibit planned under my gift, "The Price of Freedom: Americans at War." Retired General Colin Powell attended the ceremony. The exhibition covers the history of the U.S. military from the colonial era to the present. It shows and explores how war has shaped America's concept of freedom and defined its role as a world leader. Among the 700 objects in the 18,500-square-foot space are the two chairs and table used by Grant and Lee at Appomattox to sign the surrender documents that ended the Civil War; Colin Powell's woodland camouflage uniform; the nameplate from the battleship Maine; a regimental flag carried by black troops from the Civil War; a Vietnam combat "Huey" helicopter, and pieces of twisted, rusted metal from the World Trade Center, attacked on 9/11. It also includes a showcase for winners of the Congressional Medal of Honor, the nation's highest military award. The "Price of Freedom" focuses on contributions Americans have made in critical moments of our history and honors the personal sacrifices of both soldiers and civilians.

All of the exhibits include interactive stations and multimedia components to enhance the educational experience. In the mammal hall, visitors can watch a nine-minute film on evolution in a special Evolution Theater. The exhibition includes four "Discovery Zones" where visitors can use touch screens to watch videos to learn about mammal adaptations such as night vision and goose bumps. The section on Australian animals includes an interactive map with green buttons that children can push to select videos to watch.

In "The American Presidency," visitors enter the exhibition through a section titled "Presidential Campaigns," where they are greeted by a video montage of presidents on the campaign trail, and continue into "Swearing In," where presidents since Franklin D.

Roosevelt can be heard taking the oath of office. More than a dozen videos, produced in partnership with *The History Channel*, are shown continuously, including news footage and film clips on presidents in crises (such as the Great Depression and the Iran hostage crisis); there are also "home movies" of life in the White House and feature films that depict the presidents. There is even a podium that includes the Seal of the President of the United States, so young future presidents like Dev Thakar (from Chapter 7) can get a feel for the stage and pose for family photos.

And in "The Price of Freedom," touch screen computers launch first-person narratives ("My Stories"); visitors can choose from different, personal accounts that tell the experiences of ordinary men and women during times of conflict. In addition, 40 panels express individual points-of-view about the U.S. military and its role in wars and other conflicts. In one spot, visitors can sit in a reproduced living room to watch more than a dozen television sets flickering with images of the Vietnam War. At the Huey helicopter, people hear the unmistakable "whop whop whop" sound of the rotor—some soldiers in trouble called it "the sound of freedom." The Medal of Honor display features videos of recipients recounting their experiences.

And what terrific resources the Smithsonian offers on its website for teachers and students! Each exhibition, like most of them at the institution, provides teachers with online guides, lesson plans and curriculum materials, along with videos and even teaching games. In "Who Am I? A History Mystery," students select a mystery character from the Civil War and examine objects that hold the key to his or her identity. This resource was developed in conjunction with "The Price of Freedom." And the institution's separate "Smithsonian Kids" website is, as they might put it, "pretty cool!"

Perhaps to the surprise of Smithsonian officials, architects and curators, I stayed very engaged in these projects from beginning to end—I did not just sign a check, hand it over and wait for a grand opening. Throughout my business career, I led my projects and ventures. I trust my instincts, experience and leadership. As a result, while I had some setbacks and losses, I feel I was successful in business overall, from Tamarac to Blackhawk to the Seahawks. To make sure a museum comes to life with the vision I have for it, I have to be very involved, especially in the architecture, construction, floor plans and design—the areas of my expertise. It's not just that I think I can make a contribution with my leadership; I also want to make sure my financial contributions are spent wisely—on great halls and exhibitions, not wasted on unnecessary expenses or used for lots of administration and overhead.

But one thing a good leader does well is find smarter people to work with him, follow him and take leadership roles themselves. No leader can do anything alone. He is good, effective and successful only with the help of others, especially if they have a particular specialty or passion he does not. A person who creates a musical band does not have to be the best player, but he does have to know how to find and attract the people the band needs to make the music. With the Smithsonian, I could no sooner identify a top hat as Abraham Lincoln's than find the hat department at a clothing store. But the talented curators at the Smithsonian can not only determine that a particular top hat belonged to Lincoln, they can discover and use the best technology to preserve and display it for future generations. In the mammal hall alone, the renovation required the talents of 300 scientists, taxidermists and designers. (I'll offer more of my thoughts on leadership in the chapters ahead.)

All three exhibits I sponsored at the Smithsonian were well received by many reviewers, educators and museum professionals. *The New York Times* wrote of "The Price of Freedom": "It is astonishing that something like this has not been done before." *The Washington Post* said that the presidency exhibit "glows and soars with details." The *Post* called the mammal hall "awe-inspiring," noting its innovative design and the natural poses of the animal specimens. "The designers gave special attention to the needs of children," the *Post* said. "Nearly 60 percent of the visitors at the Natural History Museum are families with children under the age of 10." Reviewers from the National Park Service called the collection of specimens "outstanding" and the taxidermy "spectacular.... [It] brings them to life." As for detractors—well, at least we got them talking about important questions of nature, war and the American presidency!

But for me (and Teddy Roosevelt), it's not the critics who count. It is the people and the families who count—especially the kids.

Doug and Rebecca Manasian traveled all the way from Paw-tucket, Rhode Island, in 2012 to see the Smithsonian mammal hall for one reason: "Reality." Rebecca worried that her children, Ryan and Caitlin, spend too much time learning from a television screen. She wanted her children to have more tangible and interactive educational experiences. A trip to the Smithsonian's natural history museum was the perfect way to do this; the mammal hall in particular was a wonderful opportunity to encourage intellectual curiosity and interactive learning. It reinforced the children's interest in nature.

"Here you can see the same thing as if you went to Africa or wherever the animals are," Rebecca said. "This is true to life, real, true to scale." Rebecca hoped that teaching her children about the natural world would encourage them to interact with it with respect and caring.

Doug added that there wasn't anything like the Hall of Mammals in Rhode Island. "You don't see these types of animals in the zoo. Or you know that some of them may be extinct and not around," he said. "So obviously I wanted to show them—kind of in real life—the size of animals and some of the facts that they can learn about them. Watching TV or playing on a computer—it doesn't really give them the sense of the world anymore."

Three chapters ago, you read about Dev Thakar, who wanted to be president when he grows up. Did I mention his mom, Sejal, is an elementary school teacher? Outside of the "Price of Freedom," she said she wanted Dev and his older sister, Devanshi, to learn about one thing in particular: "Peace."

Their dad, Jig, said his takeaway from the exhibit for his children was that military men and women "have sacrificed themselves and their families to get freedom." But for Sejal, another lesson was about war's destruction: "When they read and see the actual exhibition, they will understand about the destruction and also about the things that happened and harmed the people in the past. That will inspire the children to drive their lives towards peace."

Both are good lessons for our fragile world, especially for future leaders.

Another mother, Angela Snyder, had other thoughts outside of the presidents exhibit. "This is important because you don't know where we're going unless you know the history behind our country, know the challenges that we face and the struggles that we faced," said Angela, who visited the exhibit with her twin three-year-old girls, Audrey and Brooke. "I think it's important for them. My goal for them is to create their own perspective on our country. This helps build their perspective and gives them their own perspective...I want them to grow up to know who they are and what they believe— and why they believe what they believe."

Her husband Derek added, "Thank you so much for the educational tool of an exhibit like this. You'll never know how much that does for an individual or for a kid and their future, because it may inspire them to be the next president or another great leader or another philanthropist down the line."

Brian and Brandy Slagle from Syracuse, Utah, had a specific purpose in mind when they came to Washington with two of their kids, teenagers Ethan and Brooklynn, to see "The Price of Freedom." An accountant and Army reservist, Brian was called up to active duty in 2004 to help the U.S. military set up infrastructure in Iraq. Brandy was a raised in a military family. Ethan and Brooklynn had been in elementary school while their father was deployed. They saw the exhibit as an opportunity to offer their children some perspective on their family's choices and the sacrifices they and other military families make in protecting our nation's liberties.

"I want them to be proud of the nation they live in and proud of those that gave us this nation, those that fought for it, those that served," Brandy said. But with her son Ethan thinking about a military career for himself, she—like Sejal Thakar—also wanted her children to understand "that there is a flip side to war—that a lot of times, war can be glamorized and it's not pretty, war is not pretty. I want him to look up to the heroes that have fought for our country, but I want him to understand that it comes at a great price and that there is a great sacrifice and that his grandfathers, his dad, his uncle—they all served for a reason."

For Brian, having his children understand that freedom comes at a price was important. But Brian also felt strongly that the exhibit could help develop future leaders: "To be a leader you have to understand all perspectives, you have to be able to appreciate where we've been and where we are going.... For an officer, you have to understand how to do things so you don't make the same mistakes." Brian also knew that "not everyone can be a leader, but I'd like [my children] to be leaders." Brian was glad to hear Ethan say that one of his favorite parts of the exhibit was the Medal of Honor section, "where they had someone I admire—Audie L. Murphy, for his great service in leading" fellow soldiers in World War II.

I could not agree with these parents and their kids more—which is why I am doing more—and trying to do it even better. My testing ground is China. The subject is natural history—specifically, the animal world.

After spending years in the wild in Africa and other places, I believe the animal world provides humanity with valuable lessons, especially for its future leaders. The most important of these are "survival of the fittest" and nature's awesome, humbling power to correct imbalances in the world. Man is also an animal, after all, and by observing and learning how animals survive (or don't), I believe mankind can learn how to survive.

For example, we see from the animal world how nature controls populations of species. If a species is reproducing too much, it can over-consume food supplies. The shortage of food can lead to starvation, which leads to death—and a lower population for the amount of food available. Overpopulation may also trigger the spread of disease, which can result in death and a lower population that limits the future spread of disease. Regardless, through the cycle of life, nature restores order and balance. Understanding and knowing nature's power and mechanics, I believe, can help us plan, prepare for and manage our own future as a species, especially as the world's population tops seven billion people—all of them vying for increasingly limited resources. I am an optimist about life and believe in man's capacity to find solutions to problems. But I worry that we are on a global collision course with each other and desperately need to work harder than ever to prevent a catastrophe of our own making, especially with the proliferation of weapons of mass destruction.

A wise man, Chief Seattle, chief of the Suquamish Indians in Northwest America, wrote this way about the stakes more than 150 years ago: "This we know: the Earth does not belong to man, man belongs to the Earth. All things are connected like the blood that unites us all. Man did not weave the web of life—he is merely a strand in it. Whatever he does to the web, he does to himself." Since then, the world has gotten only more populated, polluted, complicated and conflicted.

How do we survive? Look to the animals. And get kids—the leaders of tomorrow—to study them today and get thinking, because finding solutions to the world's problems is going to require a lot of it. And here's where more museums of natural history can help. They don't have to be just shrines for trophies.

With the opening of the new mammal hall at the Smithsonian in 2003, the word of my philanthropy and interests was out around the world. There was especially strong interest in China, where I had been active in business and with the Wheelchair Foundation. Multiple potential partners came calling in 2004, including museum officials in Beijing, Shanghai and Dalian. I started small that year by donating my spider collection to the Shanghai Science and Technology Museum (we had put it on display at the Blackhawk Museum before then). The museum's Spider Hall opened that December. It showcases the largest meat-eating spider on the earth, as well as a variety of other spiders from all over the world. A few live spiders inhabit the space as well, in special spider pens. The kids love it!

My first agreement for a large animal exhibition came with the Museum of Natural History in Dalian, a port city in northeast China with about six million people in the city and surrounding area. The gallery opened in 2006. It houses more than 100 specimens from Africa, North America and Eurasia and boasts a record number of large mounted museum animals, elaborate in their presentation. Each section of the exhibit has a different theme, and some even have a story line to introduce visitors to the real Africa—one tells about the food chain, starting with a lion hunting its prey.

With my donations, the Beijing Museum of Natural History opened its exhibit, called "The Beauty of Animals," in April 2007; the display was later redesigned to focus on African animals and is now called "Amazing Africa." With the help of Chinese and English drawing boards and of multimedia systems, it presents lifelike specimens in African habitats. Other features include mounted butterflies and touchable animal furs. Curators used objects I acquired from Maasai villagers to set up an entire Maasai exhibit. Now the city is planning a new natural history museum featuring these specimens and new ones.

Back in Shanghai in September 2007, the Shanghai Science and Technology Museum opened its animal hall with 170 specimens of more than 100 types of animals, including the lioness, warthog, leopard—and the hyena that little Shen Xuan found so realistic at the beginning of this chapter. Aside from the African setting, other scenes include a rainforest, wetland and artic ice field, also all wonderfully reproduced by the museum's talented designers, curators and taxidermists. The experience is enhanced by various multimedia displays.

Now Shanghai is planning a new natural history museum with even more specimens, which will be located downtown, inside the Jing'an Sculpture Park, as a branch museum of the Shanghai Science and Technology Museum. Scheduled to open by the end of 2013, it is going to be the museum of the future, integrating exhibition and education, collection and research, culture and leisure, and science and art into a whole. At one time, a museum was a little brick building with a bunch of objects stuck in it. But this museum is going to be about the objects in the building. And the building itself is also going to be a "green house" to showcase all its exhibitions in a modern and interesting way. I was told that it will be a comprehensive museum with contemporary vitality, combining the theme of "Nature, Mankind and Harmony." I believe it will represent the Shanghai standard.

Zuo Huanchen, the Board Chairman of both the Shanghai Science and Technology Museum and the Shanghai Science Education Development Foundation—and a great friend—said my donation of specimens to her museum helped speed development of the new natural history museum.

"It's important to introduce these animals to the families of Shanghai," she said. "Otherwise, kids would never have the opportunity to view such beautiful animals from around the world. But each specimen is not just about a beautiful animal—all of them were created with great detail, and each one has a story. So children can learn and leave inspired, especially about the environment and how to protect it, and how human beings can live in harmony with animals."

She added that our work in museums, education and disability in China has been helping one of the most important relationships in global affairs, the U.S.-China relationship. "Obviously China is a large country, but it is still a developing country, with a huge population," she said. "The U.S. has long been considered a developed nation, and it is in many ways it is much superior when it comes to technology, animal protection, aerospace. So I think there are many, many areas that we need to work on together, collaborate, because there are still a lot of things that we can and want to learn from the US."

"But most importantly, people like Ken know a national border really doesn't mean anything. He is a U.S. citizen, but he is doing so much in China, and I think a lot of times we need to embrace that—contribution without borders—whether it is for your own country or for another country, as long as it is for humankind. It's all very important. If we can learn to do that then it will be a much better world."

I agree, obviously. I believe China is emerging as one of the greatest countries with one of the greatest economies in the world. Its people are among the hardest-working and most intelligent in the world—and most hospitable and welcoming. Wherever I go in China, the people treat me like one of their own; many cities there have made me an honorary citizen. In geopolitics, China has matured into a strong, responsible player among developing nations, growing in influence as both a competitor and partner with the U.S. It takes this seriously—among other things, since opening to the West in 1978, it has made learning English, our language and the international language of business, a national priority for its people. Many Chinese have even taken English first names to help facilitate communication with Americans. Meanwhile, the U.S. has languished in teaching Chinese to its citizens. We surely need China as a friend as it grows its military and economy, becoming more open and innovative. It really takes several big powers to make sure some less responsible country with nuclear weapons doesn't suddenly use them to destroy half the world. With more nations seeking and obtaining such weapons, China and the U.S. can work together in friendship and cooperation to ensure peace. I hope America's political leaders work harder to accept and treat China as an equal. China has to be our ally if we are going to make a safer world.

As an "ambassador of goodwill," I am trying to do my part to strengthen our relationship by supporting more natural history exhibits in China, a physical demonstration of my friendship with the Chinese people along with our wheelchair donations—gifts from America to build bridges between our two nations.

In Beijing, Jessie Qin appreciated the gift of "Amazing Africa" at the natural history museum. She has been a docent there since 2009, after being inspired by the spirit of volunteerism in the 2008 Olympics in Beijing. She is a software consultant with a seven-year-old daughter, Annalynn. They give tours of the animal exhibit together. Their love of nature is so strong, and they found the exhibit so inspiring, that they visited Kenya in 2011 to see live animals in their natural setting in the wild. On their visit to Kenya, the tour guide refused to sit with them at first because "he said we knew everything already."

"I like the warthog because I think it is very good with family," Jessie recalled of the trip. "When we were in Kenya, the father warthog watched when the mother and the baby at the watering hole. He stood guard the whole time and waited until the mother and the baby finished, then he went himself to drink water. A very good father, a very good family."

That's just one lesson that Jessie can pass on to museum visitors. To teach kids about lions, she and Annalynn have role-played a lioness and lion cub. As the lion cub, Annalynn asks her mother a series of questions about lives of lions, from how the lioness protects her cubs to "what's for dinner?"

"My major purpose is to get the children interested in exploring the world by themselves, to add to their knowledge," Jessie said. "I want them to learn that we're only part of the whole system, no matter how important we are. Like an engine in a car, without the other parts, the system cannot work. If we lose all the other parts, the engine itself cannot survive, cannot work. This is one of the examples I use when explaining to kids why biodiversity is important, why we need to protect the biosystem...I hope we can make a difference, make people think in a different way."

It's working with her daughter. At home, Annalynn recycles bottles and tries to save on water. When they visit the park, she tells her mother not to pick flowers to protect the environment!

I want every kid in the world thinking like that. So I have been moving full-speed ahead with animal exhibits in China as part of my commitment to education and developing new leaders globally. Here is a summary of our other projects:

Yangzhou Museum

About 4.5 million people live in and around this city on the Yangtze River near the coast in China's midsection. Historically, it is one of the wealthiest of cities in China, known for its great merchant families, poets, painters and scholars. The Yangzhou Museum's "Window of World Animals" exhibit is housed in a modern new building that opened in 2005. Curators and designers integrated ecological environments, scientific education, amusement and recreation to make it come to life. The exhibit applies high-tech systems to simulate sunrise, sunset, moonlight, thunder, rain and more to enable visitors to experience the spectacle of instant weather change in nature. The exhibit adheres to the creative philosophy of harmony with nature and intimacy with animals, focusing on rare and vivid wildlife specimens to create an original ecological showcase.

Tianjin Museum of Natural History

About 13 million people live in Tianjin, a port city on the Bohai Bay in China's northeast region. It's a big city with a small-town soul. "The Animals World" exhibition opened in the Tianjin Museum in April 2007 and now features more than 200 specimens and 20 pieces of Maasai artifacts. The museum was founded and open to the public in 2004; it combined the Tianjin Historical Museum with the Tianjin Art Museum. The city has built a new natural history museum, which it plans to open in 2013. It will include two halls to display our donations. In 2011, I signed an agreement to donate more specimens for the new museum. In the new museum, visitors will be greeted by two towering figures—a polar bear and an even taller prehistoric cave bear. It is developing a story about the two animals so that kids can learn more about them, perhaps in a children's book. It also will include a large exhibit on my life and philosophy, with the objective of inspiring youngsters to dream, work hard and become successful.

Shenzhen Museum

More than 10 million people live in Shenzhen, a financial center in southeast China near Hong Kong. "Approaching The Emotional World of Animals" exhibition opened in 2012 in the new Shenzhen

Museum as a temporary one. I started there with a polar bear mount in 2009. In May 2012, I agreed to give 50 more African animal specimens. To date, I've donated more than 190. The exhibit includes an African rain forest along with a polar exhibit. Now the city is planning its own natural history museum.

Chongqing Museum of Natural History

More than 30 million people live in Chongqing and the surrounding province, a large agricultural area in south central China. A new Chongqing Museum of Natural History was scheduled to open in 2013 with a wildlife hall featuring more than 200 of our specimens in reproductions of their natural habitats. It also has about 30 items from Maasai tribes in Africa. A local newspaper wrote of the animals, "many people sighed" when they viewed them because they were so "life-like"—"fat, thin, body the proportion of each part of the muscle, etc.," but also set "in a natural posture" and "suddenly frozen" in action.

The preliminary designs for our exhibits in the new museum include a section on "Wild Africa," with a multimedia panorama of the African savannah and plains; "Survival of the Fittest" with camels and other desert animals, and an arctic exhibit with polar bear specimens. Innovative bird and butterfly displays will have creatures floating in air. The museum is also considering a "Noah's Ark" exhibit with a replica of the ark loaded with pairs of animals.

Qingdao Binhai University's Museum

The Qingdao area is home to nearly nine million people. The city is located on China's central coastline in Shandong province. The university educates 15,000 students. Its motto: "Everyone is talented, everyone is valuable." I started working with the school in 2011, donating more than 50 specimens to its nature museum so that teachers and students could better understand the relationship between man and nature and promote natural science education that stresses environmental stewardship. They went on display in 2012, when I signed a memo of cooperation with the university to contribute more specimens and enhance the exhibition. It already includes multimedia technologies with sound and light to create natural ecological landscapes that simulate an animal's living environment. A curator said one of the university's goals is to create a "jungle museum" with some of our specimens.

Shandong Museum

Shandong province, located on China's central coast, is the birthplace of Confucius. The new Shandong Museum, which opened in 2010, is located in the capital city of Jinan; it is an enormous facility with large exhibit spaces. The museum plans to showcase our specimens in two exhibition halls. In 2012, I agreed to donate 200 of them. I was impressed with the size of the new building and facilities, which will allow the museum to promote their value as educational tools. The museum will use multimedia systems to enhance the experience. It is considering a unique "tree house" for one high-ceilinged room. The house would include an exhibit on my life story that would help spread my message of natural history education and leadership. From the house, visitors would be able to survey the animals and ecosystems of the Artic, North America, Europe, South America and Asia.

Hubei Provincial Museum

Hubei, located in central east China, is known as the "land of fish and rice." The museum is in the provincial capital, Wuhan, which has a population of about 10 million people; tens of millions more people live in the surrounding area. We are working with the museum to open an animal exhibit. The museum wants to display them in the first floor of the main pavilion. In 2012, I presented the museum with Maasai artifacts, which would be incorporated in future exhibitions. I also offered to donate another 50 wild animal specimens and agreed to work closely with the museum on new projects in the future. The community may open a new natural history museum within the next few years; preliminary designs include plans for mountain, glacial, desert and grassland displays.

Institute of Zoology, Academy of Sciences, National Zoological Museum of China

The National Zoological Museum is located on the Chinese Academy of Sciences campus in Beijing. The largest zoological museum in China, it is known for its butterfly collection. We are working with the museum on plans to exhibit our animals in the main hall, in a sunken lobby on the first floor. I also have a memo of understanding with the academy's Institute of Zoology, which studies and researches biodiversity, ecology, agricultural biology, human health and reproductive biology. Its other priorities include invasive species and technological innovations for sustained control of agricultural pests.

Ningxia Association for Science and Technology, Ningxia Science and Technology Museum

About seven million people live in the Xingxia area in central China; part of the Great Wall of China runs through it. The province opened a new science and technology museum in 2008 in the capital city of Yinchuan; we have been discussing an animal exhibition there. The province is also planning a separate natural history museum.

Zhejiang Museum of Natural History

Zhejiang is another coastal province. It is the country's center of aquaculture, or fish farming—it's home to the largest fish farm in

China, in fact. The capital city of Hangzhou is home to six million people; millions more reside in the surrounding area. We are talking to the museum about setting up an animal display.

Beijing Forestry University

The university specializes in advanced education in forestry, ecology and environmental studies. In 2013, we continued discussions with administrators there about an animal exhibition.

• • •

Given the priority China has placed on education and environmental stewardship, competition for our donations is intensifying. We are talking to officials in Hong Kong and other cities about exhibitions. Officials from the Shandong Museum traveled more than 200 miles to meet me and my team in Tianjin in 2012 to discuss their ideas for a deeper partnership using their spectacular new space in Jinan. The museum is already home to one of China's richest collections of art, artifacts and cultural relics from antiquity. Now officials want to the museum to be a top player in natural history.

"What Mr. Behring has done is inspire us," said museum director Bin Wang. "He is a well-known entrepreneur and philanthropist. We admire what he has done for the Chinese people and it encourages us to do more for our own people. We are working very hard to build a world-class natural exhibition as a reward for Mr. Behring's goodwill to the Chinese people."

As with the other museums, Shandong Museum also wants to honor me with a display of photos and a timeline of my life story. (Some museums have even made bronze or marble busts and statues of me to accompany their biographical displays.) Shandong officials feel my background offers two important lessons for kids today: you can come from nothing, work hard and build a successful life. And once you've done that, you can give back.

"If you came from nowhere, you have no powerful parents and no rich family, you can still be successful," said the museum's vice director, Bo Yang. "And making money is important, but how you spend it is probably more important."

I am honored and humbled by this recognition. But the greatest honor and joy I receive is the recognition from the parents and kids who visit our exhibits, and the lessons they learn from them.

Like Cao Xafei, who traveled about 400 miles from Inner Mongolia to Beijing to see "Amazing Africa" with her son, Zhou Hongchi, 11. He loved the "fierce" crocodiles in the "fantastic" exhibit. When Xafei saw my picture at the entrance of the museum, she told her son that I was "the grandfather who donated these specimens for the creation of this exhibition." She said she is grateful to me for contributing "spiritual treasure" to the museum—something so valuable and imaginative that it cannot be assessed with numbers. The gift will help all generations—now and in the future—learn more about Africa and the environment and how human beings can live "in harmony with nature," she said.

But this is just the start. I want to give kids like Hongchi, Annalynn Zhao, Ethan Slagle, Shen Xuan and Caitlan Manasian better educations—by teaching them to think better, analyze better and be more creative. These museums are just one of the tools, one of the platforms, for the global education initiative we are building to develop the next generation of world leaders. Turn to the next chapter to read all about it...

Chapter 11
EDUCATION FOR LEADERS

Education is not preparation for life.
Education is life itself.

John Dewey

Tiger Yuan and Ryan Chang like mosquitos. At least they do now. And so do I.

Tiger and Ryan are seventh graders at the First Middle School in Qingpu District in Shanghai, China. In late summer 2012, they were participating in Global Natural History Day (GNDH) at the Shanghai Science and Technology Museum.

Before then, to them mosquitos were just bothersome pests that bite us for our blood and can spread malaria and other bad diseases. But after researching the different kinds of mosquitos in Shanghai for their GNHD project (they even built their own device to trap them), Tiger and Ryan learned something new about mosquitos: that they occupy an important place in the food chain and make critical contributions to the ecosystem. They might be annoying bloodsuckers to us, but to birds, bats, spiders and other creatures, they are a meal.

"Mosquitos are part of the biodiversity that is needed in the natural environment," Tiger told me in front of their trifold display in a hall at the museum full of other exhibits and excited students. "If we destroy the environment for mosquitos, a lot of animals will not have enough food."

To find the good in a mosquito takes a curious young mind! Tiger and Ryan will never look at mosquitos the same way again. And maybe Tiger and Ryan can do something good for the world with this knowledge someday, thanks to GNHD. It's an exciting new education initiative I started through my Global Health and Education Foundation to improve learning in the natural sciences. It is part of a new worldwide education platform I am creating to help find and develop the next generation of leaders. GNHD is designed to complement and build on the museum experience—kids see a polar bear or leopard or hyena in one of our exhibits, get interested in them and can sign up for research projects in GNHD through a local museum, which will also host science fair-style competitions.

It's called project-based learning—teaching with research projects, not just textbooks—and can be powerful. It can help kids develop critical thinking and analytical skills. Projects about nature can be especially appealing to children—what kid doesn't like animals, bugs and trees? It can stimulate and excite them about the natural world, so they can take the lessons of nature and from them to become well-educated, creative and imaginative leaders who can tackle the world's problems. Too often in China, the U.S. and other countries, schools "teach to the test"—emphasize book learning in a classroom so that kids can score well on standardized tests to advance to higher grade levels and eventually get into college. (In China, high school is like private school in the U.S.—the government only mandates education through junior high, so high school is provided to only the best and brightest students who score the highest on tests, and families pay tuition for this additional education.)

In this kind of system, teachers, administrators and parents push kids hard to excel in book learning and on exams. For Chinese parents, who are limited to one child per couple by the government, their son's or daughter's success makes them proud, of course. But it also may be key to ensuring that someone will be able to care for them in their senior years.

Whether in China or anywhere else, this kind of system tends to emphasize rote study and memorization—not critical, creative thinking. It fails to promote "out of the box" thinking that everyone, especially our leaders, needs to attack big problems like climate change, war and pollution. This kind of system can be a "fact" factory, not an "idea" factory. And it's a tunnel that is hard for some kids to escape from.

I'd been interested in improving education for many years, beginning with the teacher awards my wife, Pat, and I started at our sons' high school in Florida in the 1970s. Our outreach programs at the Blackhawk Museum made me more aware of the importance of education. I realized that many children didn't have access to the quality schools and opportunities that my sons had. Though I only completed high school, I know that my success without formal education is unusual and that I grew up in a much different world than do the children of today. Kids need a good, solid, quality education to succeed in life in these increasingly challenging times, and the world needs this so that they can take charge of at least their own lives—and sometimes lead.

One way to ensure that they get this opportunity is to support teachers, especially teachers who want to become leaders. In fact, my first major foray into education philanthropy and leadership development began with teachers. The California public school system faced (and still faces) overwhelming problems. Teachers cannot reform schools in my state without principals who promote change. So that's when I looked again to the University of California, Berkeley, in 2000 and decided to provide a $7.5 million gift to help fund scholarships for a Principal Leadership Institute (PLI) and the Kenneth E. Behring Institute for Educational Improvement. With the PLI, UC Berkeley developed a progressive program that redefines the roles of principals and creates reform-oriented leaders, committed first and foremost to improving K-12 learning in their schools. Participants take classes in school supervision, organizational policy and finances, among other courses. When they graduate, they eventually go on to become principals, superintendents, deans, supervisors, coordinators and consultants or hold other top positions in their school systems. The first class of Behring Scholars completed the program in August 2001. As of 2012, more than 400 teachers had graduated from PLI. You read about one of these impressive graduates, Marine Corps Major Nina D'Amato, in Chapter 7.

Here's another: Olga Pineda, who started her career in public education as a teacher's aide. After she became a teacher, she grew concerned about the increasing number of troubled kids she saw when she went to her school office. So she became a counselor. But she saw more and more need and became frustrated by the lack of power and resources to do something about it. That's when she applied to PLI; she graduated in 2003.

"I thought that if I became a principal, then I could help shape teachers," said Olga, who is now principal herself, at Cesar Chavez Middle School in Hayward, California. "I believe that my purpose in life is to allow students—especially immigrants and second-language kids and kids of color and underperforming kids—to have opportunities in our school system. I don't like to give up on kids. If our society is going to be a better society, then we need to invest in education, because if these kids end up in jail or homeless, what kind of future are we going to build for ourselves?"

Charles Shannon, a 2001 PLI graduate, worked on education reform in elementary schools "by taking small steps—you can't do it all at one time." As a principal, he formulated a plan for teaching kids better by recruiting people in his school who shared his vision to collaboratively plan, teach, observe, revise and share results of a "research lesson." It began to work.

"I think that oftentimes, reform becomes infectious because people see that you're doing some things that are helping kids who people didn't believe were going to make it. Those looking on start believing because they see the results. They see it in the data. They see it in the child's behavior," he said. "Then all of a sudden, other people say, 'Hey, what is it that you're doing?' until you get more and more people involved."

But Charles felt he could have a bigger impact and encourage more change by becoming an instructional leader in his school system, a literacy coach of other teachers. (As my investment in PLI shows, I think teaching teachers is a powerful way to improve education quickly.)

"It's given me a lot more time to be in classrooms, to work with teachers and focus on how to build connections with children," Charles said. "What really helps kids get motivated and feel good about themselves is when they know somebody cares. I'm glad I took charge and did something I thought was bigger than I was. I thought, 'Being a leader? Oh, wow! How scary! That's a lot of responsibility!' But it's a gradual process, and PLI laid the foundation. I'm not perfect and still learning, but at least I know I have a cohort of people who can support me along the continuum of becoming a better leader."

Cheryl Lana, a 2004 PLI graduate, ran into a challenge at a middle school where she found some teachers uninterested in professional development—making themselves better through continuing education. Two social studies teachers told her they did not need it because they had "been trained in the textbook." (Sound familiar?)

At another school, Cheryl found a better reception for new

ideas—and acted. She helped set up a pilot "intervention academic mentoring" program for 9th and 10th graders, recruiting mentors to help them with their studies.

"We went through, in a methodical way, looking at the data and making sure kids had at least one type of support," she said. "We really thought about the type of guiding questions for mentorship. We got the teachers involved and everybody felt so positive about it."

We know mentoring can have a life-changing impact on students. In Shanghai, we've been working with Johnson & Johnson's Ethicon division in a mentoring and scholarship program through its "Growing Partners" initiative in its office volunteer club. The employee club is based on the J&J credo of responsibility—first to patients and customers, second to employees and third to the community.

The company "adopted" Hexian Second Middle School in Anhui Province, a rural, mostly farm area known as the "Appalachia of China." Up to a dozen kids are accepted into the program each year based on three criteria: family financial need, grades and personal abilities. The company helps pay their tuition with partial scholarships for high school; employees mentor the students, giving them advice on academic and life issues. With their teachers, the kids visit their mentors in Shanghai twice a year. Most of the kids go on to college—evidence of the program's success.

"Our mentors teach us how to have an open mind and help us with our communication skills, how to talk to others," said Wei Zi Zi Li, 19, who loved computers and planned to study mechanical engineering. "They help us think about our future and teach us to learn not just from textbooks."

Here's what a program like this can do for a young person: The teachers told us of a girl whose mother had died suddenly; she was being raised her single dad. When Ethicon accepted her into its program, a reporter from the local television station interviewed her.

In the interview, the girl was quiet and shy and wouldn't open up. But later, when the girl was a third-year high school student, the journalist came back to interview her again—and met a completely different person! The teachers, chuckling, said the two "had a big talk" in the interview—that thanks to her mentor and the company's scholarship, the young woman was now self-confident, outgoing and headed off to college ready and prepared!

The student was not the only one that benefitted. Lydia Hua, manager of Ethicon's volunteer effort in Shanghai, said the mentors felt a strong sense of accomplishment sharing in their students' success and that mentoring encouraged them to face their own challenges each day. One employee said she discovered what volunteers everywhere learn: that you can get more out of helping others than you give.

In California, PLI graduate Cheryl Lana was a big supporter of project-based learning. I became a fan of it, too, convinced of its value through a program in the U.S. that I began supporting in 2009, National History Day (not to he confused with Global Natural History Day, which is modeled on it). I learned of National History Day (NHD) and its dynamic leader, Cathy Gorn, through the Smithsonian. My friend Libby O'Connell is the chief historian and senior vice president of corporate outreach of A&E Television Networks, which operates the History Channel. She was on the board of the Smithsonian's National Museum of American History; she was also on the board of National History Day. She wrote me a letter of introduction to Cathy that landed on my desk in Danville in 2008. Given my interest in American history, Libby thought I might be willing to support NHD, which was looking for additional funding.

I called Cathy, who has a doctorate in history, to learn more: NHD started in 1974, when 129 students from middle and high schools in the Cleveland, Ohio, area gathered on the campus of Case Western Reserve University to compete in a contest called History

Day. It was the brainchild of David Van Tassel, a history professor at CWRU. He and his colleagues were concerned by a devalued emphasis on the humanities in general—and history in particular—in the nation's schools. Van Tassel was especially critical of the rote style of learning used in most classrooms—textbook education and multiple-choice tests—and wanted to do something to reinvigorate history education.

He decided to try a contest format to motivate students to study the past—not by memorizing names and dates, but by engaging in historical inquiry and investigation. He was not interested in the spelling bee version of competition, in which students memorize information and respond to questions. Rather, Van Tassel looked to the science fair model in which students ask questions, conduct research and analyze information to draw conclusions. Based on that model, Van Tassel and his colleagues developed a History Day with competitive judging and awards.

These visionary teachers gave birth to a program that would spread nationwide and evolve into a yearlong educational experience. Now more than 600,000 kids in grades 6 through 12 and 25,000 teachers participate in History Days each year in their communities and states, culminating with an exciting national finals competition with medals and cash prizes on the campus of the University of Maryland outside Washington, DC—a kind of Olympics for history! Students compete in nine categories in two age divisions, junior division (grades 6-8) and senior division (grades 9-12):

- individual research paper
- individual exhibit
- individual performance
- individual documentary
- individual website
- group exhibit

- group performance
- group documentary
- group website.

Over the years, annual themes have included trade and industry; work and leisure; triumph and tragedy; conflict and compromise; rights; innovation and "taking a stand." Kids' projects have run the gamut from the Battle of Gettysburg and Susan B. Anthony to Navajo Code Talkers and Japanese internment camps. Students have met and interviewed former presidents Jimmy Carter and George H.W. Bush and civil rights leaders Rosa Parks and Mrs. Jackie Robinson. First-prize winners receive $1,000 to help pay for college and other expenses; seniors with top documentaries can win awards for $5,000. Top teachers can win up to $10,000. Three universities offer scholarships to students. NHD has been endorsed by the National Council for History Education, the National Council for the Social Studies and numerous other organizations. More than seven million kids have taken part in NHD.

And it has become more than just a contest. The organization sponsors workshops for history and social studies teachers, including a summer training institute, and also publishes books and curriculum materials designed to help improve student research and presentations.

What happened? How did this catch on—everywhere?

Simple. Dr. Van Tassel, Dr. Gorn (who was his assistant and became executive director of NHD in 1995) and their team knew first hand that history education in the U.S. was unpopular. When the Gallup Organization polled American adults in 2002 on which school subject had been most valuable to them in their lives, only two courses—math (34%) and English/literature/reading (24%)—scored in double digits. History came in a distant third place at 7%. Not good for our nation.

"Why do we teach history in the first place? Why we should teach it?" Cathy said. "It's to understand what's happened in the past and learn from it, to help create good citizens. That's the bottom line for us—it's about citizenship. It's about building, creating individuals who can think critically, who can analyze information, who can do research, who can draw conclusions and who can place current events into historical perspective and analyze them in such a way that they are learning from the past to understand the present and to make decisions about the future."

But note that the Gallup survey was about subjects in school, not about history itself. There's no question that Americans remain fascinated and captivated by history—just look at the popularity of our national historic parks and battlegrounds, the History Channel, historical novels and nonfiction books like the biography of John Adams by David McCullough, which was turned into a hit movie on HBO. In 2012, moviegoers swamped theaters to see Steven Spielberg's film "Lincoln."

"People don't hate history—they hate memorizing names and dates," Cathy said. "There's nothing boring about history—it's full of incredible stories. When kids study the past, they find their heroes. And they find out that ordinary people can do extraordinary things. It's ordinary citizens who've made this country what it is. It's about leadership at all levels, not just leadership in a president. Leadership by the average American citizen is what makes this country go and get better and deal with the bad things when they happen."

"But when it's taught as facts, and just facts, then it's boring and irrelevant. And students ask themselves, 'Why am I wasting my time on this?' So we wanted to change that and get kids excited about learning—not just excited about history, but excited about learning, that learning doesn't have to be sitting at a desk, memorizing stuff. Instead, with History Day, kids choose their own topic, go out and do their own research. It gives them the opportunity to take ownership of their learning and that's very important. When they choose their topic, when they map out their own plan of action, work really hard, get into those 'primary' sources, they are so much more likely to finish it, to go the distance with it.

"Letters and diaries and census records and old newspapers and oral history interviews and all that—it makes history come alive, and that inspires kids," Cathy said. "Kids get into those archives and they open up those gray boxes and they take out that yellowed paper with their white gloves on and they are thrilled! It's exciting because there it is, right in your hand—history! They're holding it right in their hands and suddenly they become so excited and they just want to tell you everything—'Look what I found, look what I found, look what this person said,' and off they go and there's no stopping them. It's the joy of discovery—of history and themselves."

"I'm in," I told her. "How much do you need?"

Along with my wife, Pat, who also loves history, I committed to funding NHD—more than $2 million so far. Pat sponsors the Patricia Behring Teacher of the Year Award, one for junior high and one for senior high, with the $10,000 prizes. We have joined other supporters that include the History Channel, Booz Allen Hamilton, Southwest Airlines and the National Endowment for the Humanities. The finals competition is now called "The Kenneth E. Behring National History Day Contest." My son David, a history lover too, is on the organization's board of trustees.

Since my family and I became involved, we have seen amazing projects from amazing kids—like Adam Dietrich, a seventh-grader from St. Peter's Catholic School in Greenville, N.C. NHD's theme for 2012 was "Revolution, Reaction, Reform in History." Nearly 2,800 finalists, along with 800 teachers, 350 judges and hundreds of parents and well-wishers, reported to the Maryland campus to compete in June that year. At his school back home, Adam had entered the junior individual performance category. In Maryland, he performed his research topic, "The Homestead Steel Rebellion, a Revolution in American Labor," before three judges and an audience. NHD chose him to give an encore of his exciting presentation at the National History Night celebration at the National Museum of American History after the final day of competition. Pat, David and I watched along with a group of NHD supporters and Smithsonian officials. By coincidence, it was my 84th birthday, and Adam's project was a wonderful birthday present—a gift of education to all of us! (Never stop learning.)

The Homestead Strike was a clash between one of the nation's first labor unions, the Amalgamated Association of Iron and Steel Workers, and Andrew Carnegie's steel company at his plant in Homestead, Pennsylvania. The strike began when factory workers refused the company's demand for a 22 percent cut in wages; the factory locked out the workers in June 1892. The dispute led to a bloody battle between the workers and private security agents a week later. The union was defeated when the governor sent in state militia and broke the strike; the loss set back the union movement for years.

With a good measure of self-confidence in front of a large audience of adults at a reception, Adam first prepared for his performance, taking time to set his props exactly right in front of a canvas depicting steel mills. Then he put on a black cap—and the show began. He announced that he came from four generations of Pennsylvania steelworkers, "a tradition of work as strong as the product we make." Next he launched into the story of the mill, its workers and the strike, using a boxing match as a metaphor for the conflict—Carnegie and his plant boss, Henry Clay Frick, in one corner and the union's leader, Hugh O'Donnell, in the other. Frick's demand to cut union pay was a punch "below the wages," Adam said.

"Wow, what a fight," he said in conclusion. "The Homestead Rebellion was possibly the darkest moment in labor history."

At the NHD awards ceremony the next day, Adam received a bronze medal for his work, winning in the junior performance category. As for other topics and contestants, a winner in the individual exhibition category explored the U.S. "Bay of Pigs" invasion of Cuba in 1961. Two winners of the group documentary category reported on Poland's "Solidarity" union uprising in 1980. A winner in research papers wrote about the medical revolution in antibiotics. And a winner in the website category received a silver medal for his presentation on the "Enigma Machine," the device the Nazis used to code and keep secret their communications during World War II— and which the Allies cracked.

Not all NHD participants win medals or prizes, but everyone's a winner. A study of more than 2,000 high school students in the 2009–2010 school year found that NHD kids outperformed their peers on multiple measures; it indicated that upward trends in performance were linked to multiple years of participation. The evaluation reported that:

- NHD students outperform their non-NHD peers on state standardized tests, not only in social studies, but in reading, science and math as well.
- NHD students are better writers who write with a purpose and real voice and marshal solid evidence to support their point of view.
- NHD students are critical thinkers who can digest, analyze and synthesize information.
- NHD students learn 21st century skills. They learn how to collaborate with team members, talk to experts, manage their time and persevere.
- NHD has a positive impact among students whose interests in academic subjects may wane in high school.

This doesn't surprise me. I've seen it for myself, when I attend NHD each year. NHD teaches students important public speaking and presentation skills. Group entrants learn how to work together, which develops their discussion, debate and negotiating skills (after all, they have to come to agreement in their projects and presentations). Kids learn how to set high standards and goals for themselves. They learn how to work hard—and the value of hard work. They have to want to do it, to put their energy into a project, to go the extra mile. NHD helps kids develop abilities for being successful in careers and in life.

Restaurateur and Food Network star Guy Fieri credits NHD in part with his success. By age 13, he was already an entrepreneur. He loved hot soft pretzels and, with his dad, had built a hot pretzel stand to sell "Awesome Hot Pretzels." But he struggled in school until a caring teacher pulled him aside in seventh grade to encourage him and told him to apply himself more. He listened, got to work, and the next year felt confident enough academically to enter the NHD competition at his junior high school in his hometown of Ferndale, California.

"I was running the Awesome Pretzel Company—it was in its heyday at the time—so I (did) the history of pretzels," he told his network in an interview in 2010. The title of his project was "The Awesome Pretzel: The History of the Evolution of Pretzels and Pushcarts As It Relates to the Awesome Pretzel Company."

He won first place in California in the junior division of his category.

"It sort of solidified in his mind that he really could do all these things that he dreamed of and planned on, that he could take on things and succeed," his dad Jim told the Food Network.

Though he had no formal training as a chef, Guy went on to open several restaurants in California after he graduated from college and worked in restaurant management. In 2006, he won the second season of *The Next Food Network Star* and was awarded a six-episode commitment for his own cooking show. *Guy's Big Bite* premiered on the Food Network in June 2006; his second series, *Diners, Drive-Ins and Dives*, premiered in April 2007. They are among the network's most popular programs.

You met Gretchen Mohr, a high school senior from Long Grove, Iowa, in Chapter 7; she has become a leader in her community in fighting hunger. She said NHD paid off for her in writing, research, and speaking skills. She has competed in the documentary category every year since seventh grade.

"History Day has put me in control of my own learning," Gretchen said. "Presenting at the competitions and sharing my projects in the community have improved my public speaking skills exponentially. My writing skills have been greatly refined as well. Whenever I have to do a research paper for school and the teacher tells the class we need a six-source bibliography, the rest of the class moans and groans while the History Day kids can do them well and quickly! Through the documentary category I have also learned a lot about working with technology and working with, meeting, and speaking to new people. The business cards I have and contacts I have made are quite extensive for an eighteen-year old from Long Grove, Iowa!"

Proud parents like Gretchen's mom, Diane, get involved in NHD activities and attend NHD competitions at the local, state and national level. They cheer on their kids and provide as much help and support as the parents of athletes do at school sports events. "For me, just getting to tag along on her journey each year has been fun and exciting," Diane said. "History Day has changed her life and opened many doors."

Gretchen's NHD coach, Christine Green, a retired teacher, started using the NHD program nearly 25 years ago in her sixth-grade class. She's still at it today at North Scott Junior High School in Eldridge, Iowa, where students come after school to work with her on their projects.

"They come in all kinds of weather, they stay into the wee hours of the morning, they work on Saturdays and Sundays, they travel hundreds of miles doing research, they interview historians and history makers," Christine said. "And less than 20 percent of these students receive credit from the school district for researching and creating a History Day project. Even those students receiving credit participated in the program before they got credit. So why do they do this? I firmly believe the answer lies in the fact this program allows students to take control of their learning. They learn because they want to learn about their topic, and in the journey, they become caught in the wonderful web of history and how it applies to their life. They experience the connections to all they have been learning in school. They learn because they want to learn! They apply their background knowledge and skills because their learning means really something to them!"

Christine said that part of each of each student's History Day journey "is the opportunity to touch history through interviews, visits to historic sites, letters, e-mails and conversations with history makers." She praised History Day as an educational tool:

> *Seeing my most reticent students converse intelligently with historians, archivists, professors, Holocaust survivors, WPA and CCC workers, civil rights icons such as Rosa Parks and Myrlie Evers, legislators, governors, business people, World Food Prize recipients, United Nations members, sports figures and religious leaders puts history and its telling in the minds and voices of a new generation. It shows students that history has a face, a voice, a smell, a touch, a meaning that can be lost in other traditional approaches.*
>
> *The program is a perfect tool for students to take charge*

*of their own education and learning experience. I, as the
teacher, am the facilitator and NOT the all-knowing
source of knowledge in the classroom. The student has
become the teacher—and his or her own advocate for
acquiring knowledge. The student is able to actively
engage peers and audiences in the joy of learning, which I
believe creates lifelong learners. The student is the owner of
the key themes and information surrounding their specific
topic, but in a greater sense, all of history. The student is
the confident individual who can teach others, which is
indeed the highest level of the learning model.*

She added, "The Behring Family's generous donation of funds,
interest and time has helped this program continue to grow and
flourish. We owe them a huge debt of gratitude for their support."

Thank you, Christine, but the honor is ours. We are overwhelmed
by the response to NHD, the impact NHD has had on young people,
and the difference it is making in our schools and to our nation. We
love attending NHD each year; meeting the kids, parents and teachers, so excited about history; stopping and taking pictures with them
as we walk through the University of Maryland student union and
other buildings to see their impressive exhibits, performances and
films; and soaking up the energy the participants and their families
radiate over the four days of final competition and awards. I've met
mothers who have had five or six children participate in NHD! (One
Smithsonian official called me a "history rock star" to the kids, who
seek me out to view their work and grab me for a photo.)

We've been moved by some of the stories from teachers and parents of how the gifts of NHD can help bring out the hidden talents of
students who otherwise appear unmotivated. NHD helps kids blossom and overcome their fears. It gives students who struggle against
the odds an opportunity to shine and be proud of their accomplish-

ments. It gives young people who face challenges at home, kids who otherwise have little support or help or who struggle to find themselves a chance to see that they can compete with the best of them, which builds their self-confidence.

A teacher from Washington State told Cathy that NHD transformed 11 students in an alternative program at her high school. These were kids who had "fallen through a lot of cracks," the teacher said. But she pushed them to participate and when they made it to the regionals, something happened:

> *All of them met me at school on time and ready to go. In fact, looking at all of the kids, extra earrings had been removed, tattoos covered up, makeup toned down, hair pulled back, and every last one of them was dressed appropriately. One student was upset because he'd purchased a white button down shirt and it was creased because he didn't know how to iron it. This young man was living on his own at age 17 and worked 40 hours a week to make rent and buy food, but he was determined to look good when he answered questions on his historical paper.*
>
> *Four of the students placed and went on to compete at state, a fact the community made quite a fuss over since our district had never competed in NHD before. After all, it was exceptional that I had been able to do something like this with those kids. The true success is that of the 11 students, seven graduated from high school, three earned a GED, and one is a sixth year senior and is determined not to give up. I have had several of that group of kids come back to visit and a couple of them are even in college. One told me, in all seriousness, that college was way easier than competing in NHD.*
>
> *I know that competing in National History Day pushed*

*those eleven students beyond the mental and academic
limits they had set for themselves and allowed to be set by
other people. They developed confidence, pride and skills
that are helping them be successful in their lives.*

Wow. A program that keeps kids off the streets, builds them up,
builds their self-confidence, builds their belief in their own abilities,
makes them successful, makes them better citizens, and prepares
them for life!

And by the way—it can turn them into leaders.

"Studying the past reveals to students that ordinary people can
do extraordinary things and that the past is about real people facing
very real conflicts," Cathy Gorn said. "By studying history, students
learn about people whose strength and determination teach them
about leadership and commitment. By uncovering the past, kids see
how average people can overcome tragedy through personal triumph, and how injustice inspires others to risk their own lives to
improve the lives of many. And, perhaps most important, students
are motivated to do as those who came before them—to become
involved, to participate, to take a stand for what they believe in, to
take action to improve their communities, their country and even the
world. Thus, students who participate in NHD are inspired by the
past and choose to take part in the world as active citizens and
leaders."

Ruth DeGolia became one. She was an eighth grader in Cleveland Heights, Ohio, when she was first introduced to NHD. She did
her project on the Abraham Lincoln Brigade, a group of American
volunteers who fought in the Spanish Civil War in 1937 and 1938.
In an article in NHD News, an organization newsletter, she said she
discovered two things by participating: first, "I was very passionate
about research and history, as well as inspiring social movements,"
and second, "how proud I was to be born in a country with such a

tradition of helping others in a very selfless way."

She participated in NHD again in her sophomore year in high school. She wanted to do a project that gave her a chance "to explore and better understand important events and movements in history related to issues I cared about, such as social justice, democratization, and human rights." She and a partner submitted a project about El Salvador.

When they won the History Channel award at the national contest, Ruth used her share of the prize money to travel to El Salvador, her first trip to Latin America, which she had only read about. In 2002, while a student at Yale University, she visited Guatemala, which had been devastated by a civil war. (The Wheelchair Foundation has delivered more than 8,600 wheelchairs there, as well as 9,000 to El Salvador.) In Guatemala she decided to help poor indigenous women overcome their poverty and circumstances. She wrote her senior thesis on the impact of globalization on political and economic development in the western highlands of Guatemala. It won the prize in her department for best thesis.

"I remember feeling that the skills and knowledge base that I developed through the NHD competition really contributed to that success," Ruth told NHD News. "[NHD] provided me with a sound knowledge base with regard to economic, political, and social issues in Central America…. This knowledge contributed to my academic success at Yale … [and] also provided me with the background I needed to set up a successful nonprofit that could help alleviate economic and social inequality in that region."

In 2004, Ruth and a Yale classmate, Benita Singh, founded Mercado Global, an organization that helps female artisans in Latin America sell their handmade rugs, jewelry and other handicrafts in the U.S. Mercado Global's sales and business support for women's artisan cooperatives have lifted families in rural communities out of poverty and supported local women's leadership.

Their work landed Ruth and Benita on the cover of *Newsweek* magazine in 2006 for an article about "Fifteen People Who Make America Great," with actor Brad Pitt and CNN anchor Soledad O'Brien. Today Mercado Global represents 400 artisans in 30 communities across Guatemala, creating products that appear in retail outlets throughout North America. About 2,000 children have been able to attend school thanks to incomes generated by Mercado Global for their mothers. You can learn more about the program at www.MercadoGlobal.org.

"We were thinking outside the box because we didn't even know where the box was," Ruth told the *Huffington Post* in 2012.

That's what I want to see in education. That's my goal with my investment in education. That's why I using the NHD model in the natural sciences, starting in China with Global Natural History Day.

Global Natural History Day is designed to inspire the interest of elementary and middle school students in natural sciences and history, to improve their analytical and critical thinking abilities through extracurricular projects, like NHD projects, that require extensive investigation. In a yearlong program, students explore local, state, national and world natural history around an annual theme, such as environmental protection. As with NHD, primary sources of information are preferred. Students conduct research through libraries, archives, museums and oral interviews. They analyze and interpret their findings, draw conclusions about their topics' significance and create final projects to present their work, supervised by a teacher or coach. Their projects can be entered into a series of academic competitions, from the local to the national level. Natural historians, educators and professionals from different walks of life review them in balanced evaluations. All types of students participate in GNHD: public, urban, suburban, rural and migrant students; English language learners; the academically gifted and students with special needs.

In early 2012, I traveled to Beijing, Shanghai and Tianjin to announce the launch of GNHD; local leaders, museum officials, educators and others joined in the press conferences. By the end of summer, more than 500 students in those cities had completed projects and were competing in performances and exhibitions, most of them in teams. They were joined and supported by many of their parents and teachers. The theme for our first year was biodiversity—the variation in life forms in species, nature and the planet.

Contest winners won a once-in-a-lifetime opportunity to go on a "Kenneth E. Behring Discovery Trip" to museums, educational and government institutions in the U.S. They first flew to Washington, DC, where they got to visit the Smithsonian, the U.S. Capitol, the U.S. Mint and other sites. Then they flew to California, to visit UC Berkeley, the Blackhawk Museum and other venues. For a little serious fun and downtime, we threw in a trip to Disneyland! Eleven winners came in all, joined by parents, coaches, teachers, GNHD supporters and members of my team—44 people in the delegation. Helen Hong, who you met in Chapter 7, was one of them; she won the top prize in in the international division in 2012. She was a contestant in Beijing with her project on the Beijing swift.

While 288 teams competed in the first year of GNHD, we feel the program had a big impact in China, with word of it reaching 4,000 schools with four million students in 50 districts and counties. Not a bad start. And it is already making a difference.

Two contestants in Shanghai, Chao Yan and Ma Ling, both fourth graders, picked macaws for their project. They were inspired by pictures of the colorful species of parrot on a website; they worried that other people might not get to enjoy the beauty of macaws because they are in danger of extinction.

"Our school has a project to raise money to feed the macaws," Yan said—that's how they first learned of the birds and looked them up on the Internet. They said GNHD offered them a chance to do

something more to help the birds. They spent three weeks researching the habits, habitats and dangers facing macaws. Their goal was
to raise awareness about macaws and the efforts to protect them. The
girls were excited to be a part of GNHD and enjoyed sharing the
information they had worked so hard to collect. They wanted to post
their project on both their school and the GNHD websites to help
spread the word about macaws. They hoped we would expand
GNHD "to promote these kinds of activities to let more people to
take part in it." They said participating in GNHD personalized environmental responsibility for them and helped foster their desire to
be good stewards of the natural world. They wanted others to experience that as well.

Yan's mother, Wei, attended the Shanghai preliminaries. She was
impressed by the amount of effort the students put into their projects
and how serious they were about presenting what they had learned.
She was proud of her daughter's achievement. She said it heartened
her to see how the day's events encouraged kids to "expand their
knowledge...do what they want to do...(and) try their best." Wei
wanted her daughter and her daughter's friends to grow up to be
leaders; she said she felt GNHD helped them with that goal because
it gave them the opportunity to develop their analytical and presentation skills while encouraging them to understand the natural
world. Wei believed that teaching children about the natural world
would lead to safer, healthier living.

"Learning how to protect the natural world so we can live safely
is important because we all live in the natural world," she said. "Mr.
Behring's idea is very good." When Wei met me, she said, "Thank
you from China."

Teachers seemed pleased with GHND, too. Ryan and Tiger's
teacher, Yuan Fang Fang, thought it was "fantastic." She was glad to
see that the project not only gave her students opportunities to do
research, but also to present their findings publicly and meet and

talk to other contestants. Yuan was impressed that the kids' presentations were structured to make sure they took full responsibility for their work. Yuan gave Tiger and Ryan the requirements for their mosquito project, but it was up to them to "do every investigation, every analysis for themselves…. They can expand their minds and their skills…. It's quite good, quite helpful." GNHD, she said, gave them room to explore, to question, and to gain abilities that will make them better leaders in the future.

Zhou Xuan, a teacher and community leader, said GNHD helped two other fourth graders, Tony Chu and Calvin Gu, with "deep thinking." Xuan helped them select two species—one plant and one animal—to research nature's balance. They chose invasive species because "a lot of animals invade China and break the balance," Xuan said. Tony and Calvin picked the American red-eared slider turtle (the common pond turtle) and a type of water hyacinth that grows so quickly it can cover entire bodies of water and stop boat travel. Although they presented their findings together under the theme of "invasion," they agreed Tony would focus on the turtles and Calvin would concentrate on the water hyacinths. They both learned the Latin name for the plant—"eichhornia crassipeds."

Tony found that the turtles were originally imported as pets, but because they'd been overbred, many owners released them into the wild. Now they have overpopulated the lakes of Shandong Province and have been muscling out the native turtles by eating all their food. In America, the slider turtle is harmless and lives in its natural habitat in proper balance with its environment. But its population in China is larger than the native turtles' and it has become a carrier for harmful bacteria. Tony and Calvin, who knew a little about this issue before their research, decided to investigate further; they hoped to convince the turtles' owners not to release them.

In his research into the water hyacinth, Calvin discovered it was imported from South America for its beautiful flowers. In the wild, its rapid growth creates dangerous imbalances in the ecosystem. The Chinese government spends money every year fighting its spread with chemicals, harvesting and the introduction of natural predators (insects, plant viruses, etc.). Tony and Calvin hope to encourage flower lovers to pick a different type of blossom.

"It's a big problem for China," Calvin said.

In just its first year, GNHD was already helping develop young leaders. Rickey Guo, an eighth-grader at Tsinghau International School in Beijing, was not only a contestant in GNHD, but he also worked as a volunteer. Using his experience as the editor-in-chief of his school newspaper, Rickey helped GNHD with newsletters and press releases. Because he learned English at a young age—it is mandatory at his school and the school's official language—he also helped translate the Global Health and Education Foundation's written resources from English to Chinese.

Volunteering is important to Rickey. It is one of the first steps in learning to be a leader—giving over your valuable time to others for free, with no expectation of compensation. It was also a first for his anyone in his family, too. He explained that the Chinese concept of volunteerism is different from the American concept. In the Chinese culture, volunteerism is related more to helping family than helping community—loyalty to parents is the honored tradition. "Charity begins at home," as the saying goes. But volunteering for GNHD made Rickey feel he was achieving something bigger, that he got a chance to give back more than he received and exceeded his own expectations of his abilities. He liked being part of something that made him feel bigger than himself.

Rickey especially liked the structure of GNHD and the opportunity for a different kind of learning than he was used to. In his school, he said, teachers dictate the schoolwork—"you study all these facts, information, data"—while in GNHD, "it's all up to us." Participants decided what they wanted to write and what they wanted to learn, and nothing got done unless they took full responsibility for it. Rickey saw this as "good practice" for growing up, when as an adult you have to be responsible for your life and use your skills to make a living.

Rickey also liked another aspect of GNHD: it was the student's choice to participate—it was open to all. He said that in China, teachers usually selected the best students for special events like GNHD based on their grades. But the way GNHD was structured, he said, any student who wanted to participate and was willing to do the work got to enter. According to Rickey, it was rare to find this type of educational opportunity in China—an "American-style" project-based academic competition. He explained that China is not yet like the U.S., where such competitions are widespread across many subject areas and an important part of the education system.

"China is like a piece of white paper with nothing on it," he said.

We want to help you and other friends in China paint it, Rickey. With the success of the first year of GNHD, we are moving quickly to set up GNHD in every city, town and province in China, the way NHD operates in the U.S., as well as in other countries. In China, most of the museums we were working with have agreed to help us with GNHD competitions in 2013—about 10 cities and regions in all. We have also started to expand GNHD—to Hong Kong, South Korea and several other nations. In the U.S., we planned on teams from Hawaii and California in 2013 and will quickly cover all 50 states. All of this will make Global Natural History Day truly global.

For our ultimate goal is to develop more Rickeys and Helens and Gretchens all around the world—students who are smart, open, energetic, engaged, well-educated, charitable, creative, caring, concerned, curious, focused, forward-looking, hard-working, enthusiastic, persevering, purposeful and selfless—the qualities of a potential future leader. We have created all the pieces for an international program that will do this. Now let me show you how they fit together.

Chapter 12
NEW LEADERS FOR A NEW WORLD

*The best way to predict the future
is to invent it.*

Steve Jobs and Alan Kay

As a builder, I know something about switches.

You walk into a room, flick a switch, and in an instant, the power surges—and a light goes on.

That's what I am trying to do with young people—who, somewhere deep down, may have a leader inside them. Flick the switch, make a light go on, bring out the leader within them—and put them on the path to their destiny.

I have written about all the programs, the tools we have assembled to do this—the museums, National History Day, Global Natural History Day. But for these kids, it is not just about learning more about mosquitos or macaws or a union strike in 1892. It's about what happens to the students when they rise to a challenge. They can take the first step in the journey to leadership by taking a chance, taking a risk and seizing an opportunity—which is what leaders do. It's an

opportunity—perhaps the first of their young lives—to test themselves, to see if they have what it takes: Do I have the brains, the
courage, the desire to tackle a question, examine a problem, dig
deep into an issue in a public competition, a contest, with no guaran-
tee of victory or reward? That's hard for anybody to do, but especially
hard for an 11, 12, or 13-year-old who fears failure or embarrass-
ment in front of classmates, teachers and parents.

But life is a competition, a contest, about "survival of the fittest."
The young people who take that first step to enter the arena, overcoming their fear, start to set themselves apart. Once they take the
first step, they take the next step, using their gifts of a good brain
and curiosity and desire to succeed at a challenge; with the support
of loving teachers, coaches and parents, they dig into a project and
start to learn and make discoveries.

This excites them, and they want to do more. They keep
researching and analyzing; they come up with more questions for
themselves and go back to find more answers. They drill down,
becoming more excited by their new knowledge, and they begin to
share it with their parents or teachers, who say, "I didn't know that—
tell me more!" And they say to themselves, "Wow, I know something
my mom or dad or teacher do not know! Maybe I AM smart!" Self-
doubt starts to fade. Self-confidence starts to build.

They get back to work, and over days and weeks, they keep working—after class and at home—doing more and more research; digging into documents, interviewing experts; growing more excited
about the possibility of sharing their discoveries! They redesign their
exhibit, they rewrite their paper, they re-edit their documentary, they
rehearse their performance or presentation over and over again—
first alone in their bedroom, then at home to their parents, then at
school to their coach or teacher. With each session, the students get
encouragement, feedback and positive reinforcement. There are
questions, of course, and criticisms and setbacks, but not enough to

stop them. They try harder, they work harder, they think harder! And as their project improves—and with each positive, encouraging, supportive comment from their mom or dad or teacher—their self-confidence grows.

Finally the day comes. They look around at the other contestants in the hall. Everybody is putting up their own exhibits now and eyeing the competition. Most students are a little nervous—they have butterflies in their stomachs. But each participant has worked hard. Each boy or girl is prepared. Each one knows his or her subject cold. Each one is ready for any question or comment from the judges. They are ready to make their parents, teachers, schools and communities proud. And each one is proud of what he or she has already accomplished. They are confident in their knowledge and their ability.

They have already won.

Even if they don't have the right answers for the judges, at least they have gone through the process to get there. They can learn from failure as much as from success and they will be better for having tried. Even if they don't win a gold, silver or bronze medal or a certificate, even if they do not advance to their state or province competition, even if they do not get to the national finals, they have won. By simply choosing to enter the arena, by seizing a chance and taking it, they are all winners.

We can grow leaders with that and take it to the next level, all of us together—so that the world can win, too.

Every child can build self-confidence in this kind of exercise. But more important, learning about something new—mosquitos, pretzels, disability—can trigger passion about a subject, an issue, a problem, a challenge, a field—which can lead to purpose. Then bigger things can happen that can help make the world a better place. Living for a purpose—a passion for something—gets someone's juices going, gives an individual extraordinary energy, keeps him or her—child or adult—excited and makes them unstoppable in their pursuit of an idea, a goal, a dream. Then that person can lead a charge, and their passion, energy, desire and hard work begin to attract attention—and then maybe others begin to follow.

Every leader needs followers—donors, employees, volunteers. A leader is good and successful only if he has followers. I don't use that word in a derogatory or belittling way. Not everyone can be a leader; a person may not have basic requirements for leadership, such as a burning desire to get something done. Many people don't want to be a leader because it can be hard and takes a lot of time, work and responsibility. They also may fear the inevitable attacks from the "destroyers" in life—those who, because of anger, bitterness, jealousy or resentment, seek to block or tear down leaders and causes. That's OK—it can be good, fun and rewarding to be a follower. But a leader alone is worthless—nothing. I could not have done anything in business or philanthropy for all these years if I did not have good, excited people helping me. And we did some amazing, wonderful things together—like delivering nearly a million wheelchairs to physically disabled people in 150 countries around the world in little more than a decade, for starters. Thank goodness for followers!

But we have a shortage of leaders in the world. We desperately need more leaders to tackle the world's problems, which are only getting more difficult, demanding and complicated.

The dictionary defines a leader as "a person who rules, guides or inspires others." That's a start. Others have added that leaders are the ones who break the rules and push to the edge, who are not satisfied with things as they are. They don't work 15 hours a day because they have to, they work 15 hours a day because they want to! They don't get into something because they have to have a job, they get into something because they want to create a new reality.

But to me, leadership really begins with ideas. How do you rule, guide or inspire anyone without ideas? How do you get anyone to believe in you? Ideas matter. Big ideas are behind some of the most powerful, positive forces in human history: religion, peace, freedom, self-government, education, innovation and free enterprise.

I like big ideas; there are 100 million physically disabled people in the world who need a wheelchair but cannot afford one. Let's start a charitable organization to give them free ones. The California school system is failing and its students are at risk. Let's teach teachers how to fix it. Those who do not learn the lessons of history are doomed to repeat them. Let's reinvent history education for kids. The natural world offers us lessons that could save humanity. Let's reinvent natural history museums and learning.

Now, because mankind needs more leaders, let's come together around a global program to find and develop young people who could become one—a program that challenges and excites them with demanding activities that develop critical leadership skills, allows them to discover the leadership potential within themselves, gives them a chance to prove something to themselves, provides them with opportunities to learn from and be inspired by our current leaders from all walks of life and helps them find mentors. We've already got the building blocks for this platform in the U.S. and China. We have strong relationships with outstanding educational institutions—museums and universities like UC Berkeley, the Smithsonian Institution and all of the museums I am working with in China. We are founders and supporters of outstanding education programs—Global Natural History Day, National History Day and the Principal Leadership Institute. The potential synergy of these groups is huge.

They are already starting to work together. Museums in China are supporting and hosting Global Natural History Day, contributing venues for kids' exhibits and performances. In the U.S., the University of Maryland does the same by hosting the finals of National History Day. The Smithsonian's National Museum of American History hosts the annual final celebration of NHD with National History Night, where winning students present their exhibits and presentations.

That's a good network to build on. Let's imagine stronger partnerships that help improve education for kids around the world through project-based learning—and help us find and develop the next generation of world leaders. How much impact could we have together if museums heavily promoted Global Natural History Day and provided it with armies of volunteers to help with staffing, judging and outreach to schools? What if we took graduates of Principal Leadership Institute and offered them additional, advanced degrees in leadership training to teach our top contestants—and other teachers? Our cities are full of charter schools that focus on a core discipline such as math, science or the arts—why not create charter schools that focus on leadership?

I am ready to lead in this vision with a new venture, the Behring Leadership Academy.

It has its roots in my biography. As a result of my business success and philanthropy, I began receiving some national recognition. I am particularly proud of an honor I received in 1989. One night in June, I found myself with 400 other guests and students seated at tables in a ballroom in San Francisco. I felt a bit out of place, sitting with Oprah Winfrey, George Lucas, Tom Brokaw and Ralph Lauren and the other famous inductees into the American Academy of Achievement. They must have been wondering, "Who is this man? Why is he here?" More than one mistook me for Alfred Hitchcock, who had died nine years earlier (perhaps to their surprise, I would later become president of the Academy).

The Academy of Achievement was established in 1961 to, according to its mission statement, "inspire youth with new dreams of achievement in a world of boundless opportunity, to broaden the recognition of men and women of exceptional accomplishment in

America's great fields of endeavor, to champion the spirit of free enterprise and equal opportunity for all, and to foster an international spirit of understanding by annually bringing together the great minds and talents of other nations."

Each year, over a long weekend, the Academy brought together hundreds of America's brightest high school students with men and women who have distinguished themselves in their respective fields—business, the arts, science, education, government and sports. It provided young guests with two days of one-on-one introductions, conversations, conferences and networking with Academy members. At the end, new inductees were recognized at the "Banquet of the Golden Plate." General Douglas MacArthur, Neil Armstrong, Steven Spielberg, Michael Jordan, Gerald Ford and Bill Gates are just a few leaders who have received the Golden Plate over the years. Each of them was an outstanding leader in his or her field. Each has touched the lives of many and made the world a better place.

I sat in the ballroom looking at the 40 members of my class. They included Ernest and Julio Gallo, Ralph Lauren, Tom Selleck and Steve Wynn. As I considered the list of current and former recipients of the Golden Plate, it struck me that while there was diversity in age, careers, accomplishments and interests, there was one quality that each recipient shared: All were leaders who had inspired others to believe in them. They did that with vision and credibility. They could imagine what others could not, and they had the ability to inspire others to support their ideas and enlist in their cause.

The Horatio Alger Award also recognizes this spirit. I was honored to receive it in 2006. It is named after the famed 19th-century author who wrote popular stories of young people overcoming adversity and succeeding through perseverance and by adhering to good moral principles. The organization behind it, the Horatio Alger

Association of Distinguished Americans, "is dedicated to the simple but powerful belief that hard work, honesty and determination can conquer all obstacles," its website states. "[It] continues to educate our nation's young people about the economic and personal opportunities afforded them by the promise of the American free enterprise system." The association estimated that by the end of 2014, it will have awarded $100 million in scholarships to nearly 20,000 high school students for their college expenses.

Alger wrote about achieving the American Dream. The award was established in 1947 to dispel the belief among the nation's youth that this dream was fading. As was clear from America's postwar economic boom and emergence as a superpower, that notion was not true back then, and it is not true today. Moreover, the American Dream has become the world's dream—the free-market capitalism established and advanced by our nation's visionary founders and leaders became the hope of the world, imitated far and wide and doing more to lift people out of poverty and promote individual liberty than any other economic system devised by man. Today, the best and brightest from every nation beat a path to our shores to enroll in our universities, to apply for our citizenship and to seek opportunity in the world's greatest economy.

This system has also created more wealth than any other system —wealth that has led to more and more generosity with each generation.

I am also proud of my membership in another organization 70 years ago: the Boy Scouts of America. As a kid in Monroe, Wisconsin, I was a member of Troop 114. As much as any other group, the Boy Scouts helped to shape me though its program to build character, responsible citizenship and personal fitness, laying the foundation for my life. I can still recite the Scout's Law: "A Scout is trustworthy, loyal, helpful, friendly, courteous, kind, obedient, cheerful, thrifty, brave, clean and reverent." The organization's program for younger boys, the Cub Scouts, teaches 12 "core values" that underscore this creed; they include cooperation ("being helpful and working with others toward a common goal"), a positive attitude ("being cheerful and setting our minds to look for and find the best in all situations") and resourcefulness ("using human and other resources to their fullest"). In Chapter 9, you read how scouting can help put young men on the path to leadership with the story of Justin Gonsalves, who started raising money for the Wheelchair Foundation for an Eagle Scout project. H. Ross Perot, Sam Walton, Bill Gates and many other prominent business leaders were Scouts; so were presidents John F. Kennedy and Gerald Ford (presidents Bill Clinton, George W. Bush and Barack Obama were Cub Scouts). In 2012, nearly half the members of Congress were Scouts or Scouting volunteers. Baseball great Hank Aaron was a Scout, as was Dr. William Devries, who transplanted the first artificial heart, and actor Jimmy Stewart ("I wouldn't trade my experiences in Scouting for anything"). Since its founding in 1910, more than 100 million boys and young men have participated in Scouting, encouraged by more than 30 million adult volunteers.

The Girl Scouts, Junior Achievement, 4-H, Future Farmers of America and Boys and Girls Clubs are other prominent organizations for young people. They all do basically the same thing—provide kids with positive guidance and extracurricular activities during their formative years. They teach them good core values that can help them realize their full potential as responsible, productive, caring adults and citizens. These values should be as relevant, helpful and powerful for current and future generations as they were for my generation and me. And I see no reason why they should not be promoted to young people everywhere today, whether or not they are Americans. We should all try to teach these values and live by them every day as citizens of the world.

I believe my leadership academy will incorporate the best

features of all of these organizations and will be even more effective through partnerships with National History Day, Global Natural History Day and others. I think my academy could be "more, better and different." I want my programs to stay focused on middle and high school students as opposed to, say, the Academy of Achievement, which now concentrates on graduate school students. I see my academy offering advanced classes in leadership to winners of NHD and GNHD each year; to top Boy Scouts, Girl Scouts, Junior Achievers and Future Farmers of America; to young physically disabled people who have received a wheelchair from the Wheelchair Foundation and because of it have been able to attend school and excel; and to other students of accomplishment and merit from around the world. The program could start with museums and GNHD, with kids earning their way to acceptance into my academy through their competitions and awards. Classes could be taught by PLI graduates who get our extra training; sessions could be held on a university campus. To spread the mission, the academy could develop curricula that schools in the U.S., China and around the world could use to teach leadership skills in their classrooms. We could offer books, training materials and other publications, including guides for projects in leadership that embrace project-based learning.

For the most promising students, we'd hold an annual conference of "Behring Fellows," a young leaders' summit where they could meet, speak to, learn from and be inspired by current world leaders from every field—business, government, education, science, art, entertainment, sports, religion, philanthropy—people who became successful because they "played the game from the heart." Current leaders would talk about their lives and their paths to purpose and leadership. They could each make formal speeches at the gathering, but would also get to talk to the kids informally, one-on-one. We would ask top companies to provide corporate sponsorship for this prestigious event and perhaps help us create special awards, scholarships, exchange programs and internship opportunities for our junior leaders. We think parents would highly support this effort—how many moms and dads would be proud that their child is in leadership school, with training to become a world leader? Every one! And the event could create great networking opportunities for kids and leaders—the Academy of Achievement and the Horatio Alger Association introduced me to people I would have never have met otherwise, and I am sure the students who attended their events felt the same way. You make friends at them who can become friends forever; you can help each other accomplish great things down the road.

Younger participants could also find mentors, and older ones could become one. One of the priorities of my academy would be mentoring programs, to supplement the more structured programs and the peer-to-peer learning experience that the kids would get from each other at our events. I did not have many mentors growing up; candidly, I can't think of any. I don't believe I was terribly disadvantaged by that, and I think it probably made me more independent and self-reliant. It gave me stronger self-confidence and belief in my own ability. But as I reflect on 70 years of hard work on my own and as I have expanded my philanthropy to programs for young people, I think perhaps my journey might have been helped when I was younger by words of wisdom and encouragement from time to time from more people with more business and life experience. They might have helped me avoid mistakes.

I was fortunate that I did not miss out on mentors altogether. In Ft. Lauderdale, developer Jim Hunt taught me, "never take both hands off the pump." One of my mentors in philanthropy is King Juan Carlos of Spain, who has become a good friend. He has introduced me to many people. He has given me insight into world problems and what needs to be done to create a more friendly and peaceful world. I've also been privileged to meet and learn from

Nelson Mandela, former French President Valery Giscard d'Estaing, Mikhail Gorbachev and other leaders. They greatly influenced me by demonstrating some of the qualities needed for leadership and how to deal with the events that change your own life and the world.

Here's one quality I have seen in some leaders: Many came from nothing and became something. I grew up in poverty in the Great Depression. I believe that experience gave me drive—more drive than my family members, friends and peers in business. I wanted to escape that life and never return to it. As a result, my childhood experience made me hungry for personal and financial success. I worked harder and took more risks than most people because I had nothing to lose—and I reaped the rewards. My poverty served me well. When you learn the hard way, it can be the best way…

For one thing, I never became entitled. I worry our entitlement culture today is hurting some people's—and our nation's—growth and success. I am not talking about temporary assistance that may help someone who is out of work or down on their luck for a short period—aid that gives them time to recover and get back on their feet, a hand up. I am not talking about legitimate assistance for the mentally or physically disabled or the elderly, such as Social Security, which most seniors paid into when they were gainfully employed. I am not talking about being cruel or uncaring to our neighbors who are truly helpless or in need. I am talking about government benefits that can become ongoing——policies and programs that disincentivize able-bodied people from pursuing honest work by giving them payments or benefits for long periods of time—a handout. I am especially concerned about people who take advantage of that system—and of hardworking taxpayers—because they don't want to work. It is bad enough if they are lazy, unmotivated or too proud to work. But it is especially bad when entitlement programs unintentionally destroy a person's innate desire for work and success—the hunger, the fire. And entitlements don't have to be gov-

Getting started on my journey to supporting education, with Pat and I honoring teachers at our boys' school in Florida, Pine Crest, in 1974.

My next big education venture—my donation to open the Principal Leadership Institute at the University of California at Berkeley in 2000.

The PLI has more than 400 alumni, each one doing his or her best to improve education in California. (Courtesy UC Berkeley)

The Marine Corps selected Major Nina D'Amato, a former teacher and a graduate of the Behring Principal Leadership Institute, to help rebuild schools in Afghanistan after the U.S. took control of the country after terrorist attacks of 9/11. (Courtesy UC Berkeley)

Here is Major D'Amato at one of her schools in Afghanistan.

In 2009, Pat and I began to support National History Day, a project-based competition that helps bring history to life for junior and senior school students in the U.S.

Kids just love National History Day and the contest finals that I sponsor now at the University of Maryland. (Courtesy National History Day)

Some National History Day participants compete with exhibits. Here are some from the finals at the University of Maryland. (Courtesy National History Day)

But students can also compete with performances about their projects, acting out roles of people who witnessed historical events. (Courtesy National History Day)

I especially enjoy handing out the awards and prizes for National History Day and meeting the dynamic participants and their teachers, coaches and parents. (Courtesy National History Day)

Dr. Cathy Gorn, executive director of National History Day, accepted the National Humanities Medal from President Barack Obama in 2011. (Courtesy National Endowment for the Humanities)

Do you think kids in China might get excited about research projects, too?

National History Day in the U.S. has been so successful that we used it as a model for creating a project-based competition about nature and the natural sciences, Global Natural History Day. We launched it in China in 2012.

Beijing museum and education officials welcomed the launch of Global Natural History Day at the Beijing Museum of Natural History.

My good friend, Madam Zuo Huanchen, Board Chairman of both the Shanghai Science and Technology Museum and Shanghai Science Education Development Foundation, joined me with other officials at the Shanghai launch of GNHD.

Kids in Tianjin seemed excited about GNHD.

I was pretty excited about GNHD at the Shanghai preliminaries!

As with contestants in National History Day in the U.S., participants in Global Natural History Day can create exhibits and defend their research to tough judges. These girls did a project on ladybugs.

Or students can present their research findings through performances and also face the judges.

The students jump in to their exhibits, presentations and performances!

Just what I want to see—young minds studying how to limit pollution.

A team of local leaders sat with me to judge the finalists in Shanghai in 2012.

I joined the winners on stage. The top students won a "Kenneth E. Behring Discovery Trip" to the U.S. that took them to San Francisco, California; Washington, D.C., and Disneyland.

I loved awarding the medals and prizes.

I also support many other nonprofit projects. A member of my China team facilitated a student mentoring program with employees of Johnson & Johnson in Shanghai. Mentoring will be a big part of my Behring Leadership Academy.

I have supported literacy programs. Here I am delivering books in South Africa in 2011.

I am working with Lions Clubs to provide free cataract surgeries to people with poor vision around the world. We opened this operating theater in Monterrey, Mexico, in 2010 with the support of the Walters family.

My "Safe Drinking Water" project is installing clean water technology, starting with pilot projects in China.

Global Health and Education Foundation— Creating Leaders Young and Old

In Beijing, Jessie Qin and her daughter Annalynn are leaders at the Museum of Natural History, where they give tours of my animal exhibit to kids and parents. They have played lions—Jessie as a lioness and Annalynn as her cub. They were so inspired by the exhibit and love animals so much that they traveled to a preserve in Kenya to see them in the wild for themselves.

Rickey Guo of Shanghai is well on his way to becoming a leader because of participation in Global Natural History Day and his volunteer work in our China office.

National History Day contestant Gretchen Mohr is helping to fight world hunger by organizing and leading hunger summits in her community in Iowa.

Here are the 2012 winners of Global National History Day at the National Museum of Natural History in Washington, D.C., one of the stops on their Discovery Trip. They are some of China's future leaders.

Helen Hong was on the Discovery Trip for winning first place in the international division in the 2012 GNHD. Her project was on the endangered Beijing swift. She has started a foundation to help save it.

Dev Thakar of Fremont, California, stood at the mock podium at my U.S. presidents exhibit at the Smithsonian's National Museum of American History. He wants to be president some day. If he is elected, he likely will be the first person with parents from India to do so. I'm glad the exhibit is helping to educate and inspire leaders of the future.

Brian and Brandy Slagle from Syracuse, Utah, came to Washington, D.C., to show two of their kids, Ethan and Brooklynn, the military exhibition I sponsored at the Smithsonian, "The Price of Freedom." The parents hoped it would help teach them about leadership as well as other lessons.

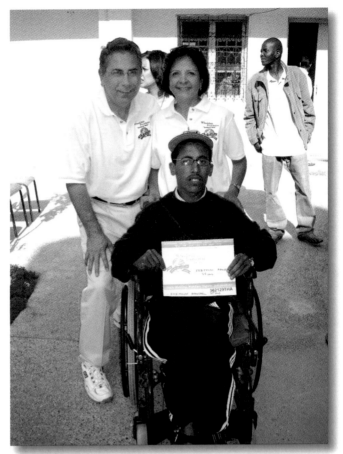

Val and Belia Nunes of Oakland, California, are leaders among our volunteers at the Wheelchair Foundation. Here they are delivering wheelchairs in Morocco. They also help us with fundraising.

Gordon Holmes, owner of Lookout Ridge Winery in Glen Ellen, California, does, too. Here he is in Ghana helping physically disabled people.

How many leaders do this? Wheelchair Foundation volunteer Josh Routh, who is himself in a wheelchair because of cerebral palsy, being carried to a distribution in Panama in 2009 by natives of a remote village in the jungle accessible only by canoe. His devoted dad, Don, is always with him on wheelchair distributions, for which they raise the funding.

The stories of these leaders—these global citizens—these people of purpose—have inspired me. I want to keep them and the causes that we believe in going. That is why I am actively managing my investments to ensure my philanthropy continues.

I have been honored my whole life for my philanthropic work. Brigham Young University awarded me an Honorary Doctorate in the Humanities in 2002.

I am an honorary citizen of Tianjin as well as other cities…

And been given many other accolades and awards…

But my greatest reward has been to find purpose in fostering good health, education, and mobility—and finding our world's future leaders.

ernment benefits—they can be handouts or inheritances from family. Like drug addicts who claim the first hit won't hook them, good people can get hooked on handouts and will stop trying.

Some leaders also believe in a higher power, which they feel helped them succeed. I do. Two religious leaders I have met, Pope John Paul II and his counterpart in the Greek Orthodox Church, His All Holiness Ecumenical Patriarch Bartholomew, believe in God, of course. Many wheelchair recipients tell me they thank God for their gift. I am not sure whether the higher power is God or not, but I have faith in it. As my life progressed, I became more and more convinced that a higher power was watching over me, signaling new opportunities for me and perhaps even keeping me alive to keep working. For some critical life events, I have no other explanation. This feeling began when I was growing up in Wisconsin and survived early brushes with death—remember that car that hit me and nearly killed me when I was 10? Remember that boat explosion that nearly killed me when I was 26? Were guardian angels watching over me? Later, I had some close calls on hunting safaris in Africa. More recently, as I have become older, I have been hospitalized for health problems, including one that left me in a coma. Yet each time I have survived, come back and received even more opportunities in my business and philanthropic work, with one door after another opening for me. In China, for example, I started donating animal specimens to natural history museums. The next thing you know, my team and I have created Global Natural History Day, to help develop critical research, analytical and thinking skills in projects about the natural world. Future leaders will need these skills to protect and save our planet. I can only conclude that this higher power has been helping me and keeping me alive for a purpose, to keep going. I accepted these gifts and resolved long ago not to squander them. I don't advocate any particular religion—I don't consider myself very religious and I have no evidence to prove the existence of a higher power. But I do urge people young and old to keep an open mind about it and consider that some events in life may not be the result of chance. If an opportunity arises that you can't explain, you may not want to spend a lot of time trying to figure out where it came from. You may just want to accept it and act on it. That's what I learned to do.

Whatever the source, one of my many blessings has been great financial success. Now I have committed a substantial portion of my wealth to my Global Health and Education Foundation, to continue to fund the philanthropic programs that reflect my vision, my mission—my purpose. I began my career as an entrepreneur, first in cars and then in homebuilding and sports, as an owner and operator of companies. I created substantial assets and income, and I operated and managed them for decades. After selling my football team, I began to diversify my assets. I invested not just in stocks, but also in private equity and buyout funds, which acquired companies like Burger King, Dunkin' Donuts and Hertz Rent-A-Car. My fellow investors included other successful people, but also pension funds and endowments with specific missions; they sought income for retirees or for important causes. I have been a diligent investor, careful with my money, building a sound portfolio, working seven days a week to find the best investments for a sustainable endowment for the causes I believe in. I finally bought a Bloomberg financial terminal and even an iPhone (my grandkids are impressed) to help me with my research. I wake up every weekday in California before 3 AM to watch financial news networks three time zones away in New York to prepare me for the trading day. As a result, my endowment includes stocks in big global companies with strong brands, balance sheets and income. Remember the spider collection I donated to the Shanghai Science and Technology Museum? Well, now I have also invested in financial instruments for diversification called "SPIDERS" because they have many feet in companies, industries and countries that I believe will grow and prosper in years to come. I want funding from interest, dividends and capital appreciation for my causes to continue in perpetuity.

At their most basic, my causes have been about trying to help people better themselves with a hand up. It can be with a wheelchair so they can go back to school, back to work or open their own business—so they can be a productive member of their family and community. It can be with a university graduate program to help teachers improve education in their communities. It can be with an exhibit at a museum that inspires children to learn more about the natural world and do something to help save it, like recycling plastic bottles. It can be with a competition for research projects about history that excites students in their classes and helps them learn the lessons of history and leadership.

But it starts with desire—and what happens next depends on it. No gift of mine, or anyone else's, will lead to great things without a desire on the part of the recipient to do something great with it. At a minimum, I hope these gifts will help create better citizens of the world, informed about the lives of men and all living things, so that people at the least can be better stewards and guardians of their freedoms and opportunities, families and communities, environment and planet. It takes looking beyond the repeating cycles of life, politics and economics to create a new, different kind of cycle—a sustained, uplifting cycle of giving and service. I hope to be the spark: that through a gift of mobility and independence, or of knowledge and learning, and witnessing what can become of it—the joy that it can create and the difference it can make—others will desire to do more, to give more. And recipients will desire to become givers themselves—now that they are better, they will turn around and help others in trouble, sorrow, sickness or in need.

This is a cycle that helps make the world better.

Learning to give back is one of the most important lessons in leadership—perhaps the most important first step on the journey to leadership. From this group of people—people of purpose—leaders will emerge. I will do all I can in my power to help find them and help them grow, to help young people discover the leaders within themselves and then nurture them until they are ready to take their place among leaders of history.

Those like Nina and Josh, Dev and Helen, Tony and Calvin, Rickey and Ruth, who would be called into Teddy Roosevelt's arena, to strive gallantly and to dare greatly—who do not fear big ideas, big deeds and getting back up when they are knocked down. Those who would be called to selfless service for the world, to help make it clean and healthy, peaceful and prosperous—to help make it better for all.

We need them.

We place our hopes in them.

Let's go.

Epilogue:
FINDING YOUR PURPOSE

The purpose of life is a life of purpose.

Robert Byrne

In October 2012, in the middle of our Global Natural History Day competitions in China, we received an email from the mother of Helen Hong, whose project was about the endangered Beijing swift and who started her own foundation to help protect them:

> *I really want to thank you for getting Helen involved in GNHD and helping her every step of the way. GNHD provides a great platform for the curious and eager mind to explore the history of the natural world. As Helen's project unfolds, she manages to confront the ups and downs of searching for ideas, developing perspectives and revising her project over and over to make it better. In the end, she comes away with a better understanding of the essence of biodiversity and the importance of balanced acts to build a*

healthy and sustainable environment. Most of all, it
inspires her to go beyond and explore her own path. GNHD
catalyzed her desire to start the Swift Action Foundation
for further effort on issues she cares deeply about.

Best regards,
Michelle Liu, Helen Hong's mother

I get letters, notes and emails like this all of the time. They rein-
force and recommit me to the purpose in my life, to the path I have
chosen, to working harder to be a good leader.

How do you find your purpose? Very simple: Open your heart
and listen to it. It's not hard. Try it right now: Can you feel in your
heart if something is missing in your life? Do you feel incomplete?
Do you have all the material possessions you want but still feel
unfulfilled, feel no joy? Then that is a powerful clue that you have
not found your purpose—and that you need to start looking for it.
That's the way I felt for most of my life.

I don't know why I do some of the things I do. I just do them.
Something affects me and I react. To find your purpose, ask yourself,
"What affects me? What breaks my heart when I see it? What
strikes a nerve?" Then follow that feeling to some course of action.
Once you act, if you feel a sense of joy, of pleasure, of satisfaction, a
feeling you have never felt before, then you have found your purpose.

Duty is not purpose. Many people do things out of a sense of
duty. I helped my parents financially later in life because, as their
son, it was my duty. Many people give money to charitable causes
because they think it is their duty, "the right thing to do," not
because of any pleasure they get from it. That's okay, because that
helps a lot of charities raise money for good causes. But to me, it's a
shame. I say this not to be critical of anyone but to try to inspire oth-

ers to look beyond their own wants, to act out of a sense of selfless service—something that took me almost a lifetime to do. I've since learned that my greatest joy has come from giving. Even if the only thing you get back is your own satisfaction or a bit of recognition, nothing compares with the feeling of knowing that someone else's life is a little better because of your effort. My greatest regret is that it took me most of my life to figure this out.

It's hard for me to ever feel any real contentment, because I am never satisfied. For every person that we help, there are millions more in need. I see millions of arms reaching up for help, billions more looking for strong leadership. The real legacy I hope to leave is to get more people helping other people and more leaders to emerge, so that after I'm gone, the work I've done will continue and will not have been in vain.

I started on my road to purpose with a wheelchair given to a physically-disabled man in Romania. Then I dreamed about possibilities. Now, more than a decade later, the Wheelchair Foundation has given birth to a larger humanitarian organization, the Global Health and Education Foundation, with bigger goals of improving the health, education and mobility of people around the world and, in the process, helping find and develop the next generation of leaders for our fragile but hope-filled planet. I have seeded GHEF with my own substantial assets and believe it will be sustained for as long as mankind needs it, with the help of other donors and organizations—and, most important, by ordinary people from all parts of the world.

I like the life that I've created. I achieved great wealth in worldly goods in my eyes and in the eyes of the world. I achieved the ultimate dream of that poor boy from Wisconsin by owning my own jet, a football team, a large yacht, several large homes and a great classic car collection, and by traveling the world and associating with famous people. I felt I was indeed rich.

But in truth, I was neither fulfilled nor satisfied with my life. Something important was missing. I know now that I did not really know what being poor was—and I did not know what being rich was. On my own road to leadership and purpose, I learned that I received joy from giving hope, freedom and dignity to some of the poorest, most unfortunate and forgotten people in the world. The most joy I've experienced has come from doing something good for someone else—especially when that person wasn't expecting it.

You don't have to be rich, own big houses or planes, travel or know famous people to do something good for someone else. You can start out small, like I did—with one wheelchair for one person, one act of kindness for one person, one smile for one person, maybe just once a month or with just 1 percent of your time. Who knows—perhaps you'll end up helping millions of people, as I did.

With purpose like that, with the help of great leaders, I believe we will change the world.

Appendix A:

KENNETH E. BEHRING,
HIGHLIGHTS OF ACHIEVEMENTS
AND AWARDS

1960's–mid-1970's
- On April 23, 1963, was granted city charter for Tamarac, Florida, a city with no residents. Today, Tamarac has about 60,000 residents.
- Developed the very first "condominium community" in Florida, and received the very first condominium financing.
- Secured two new bank charters.
- Supported building construction and *Behring Outstanding Teacher Award* programs at Pine Crest School in Ft. Lauderdale, Florida.
- Named General Electric Co. *Builder of the Year*.
- Largest builder of single family homes in the state of Florida for a half-decade and among the 10 largest home builders in the U. S.
- Sat on the boards of numerous banking institutions and other organizations, as well as the Council of 100 Top Business Leaders in Florida.

1970's–Present
- Established the Museum of Art, Science and Culture at the University of California, Berkeley.
- Established Kenneth E. Behring Institute for Educational Improvement at University of California, Berkeley, and the Principal Leadership Institute, which has developed and graduated

more than 400 principals and other educational leaders with specific focus on serving and reforming inner-city schools.

- Inducted in to the California Homebuilding Foundation *Hall of Fame* in 1992.
- Owner of the largest classic auto collection featuring coach-built automobiles at the Blackhawk Museum.
- Owner of the Seattle Seahawks National Football League franchise for nearly 10 years.
- Bay Area Sports Hall of Fame inductee, 1994.

International Honors
- 1991, '95, '97 Forbes 400 Wealthiest Americans.
- Academy of Achievement Inductee 1989. President (five year tenure).
- Rotary Hall of Fame.
- Horatio Alger Association of Distinguished Americans, 2006 inductee.
- Received Albert Einstein bust, awarded by Science and Engineering Foundation, Washington, DC.
- Board Member of China Disabled Foundation (China Disabled Person's Federation).
- 2011 *International Public Health Hero*, University of California, Berkeley, School of Public Health.
- Recipient of the *James Smithson Award* presented by the Smithsonian Institution, Washington, DC, for the preservation of America's heritage.
- American History Museum at Smithsonian Institution, Washington, DC, renamed "Kenneth E. Behring Center," and rotunda named "Kenneth E. Behring Family Hall of Mammals" at Smithsonian's Natural History Museum, Washington, DC.
- Primary sponsor of *Kenneth E. Behring National History Day Contest* with more than 600,000 student participants annually.

- Benefactor of Behring Senior Center and Monroe Theater group buildings, Monroe, Wisconsin.
- Board Member, University of Wisconsin, Athletics.
- Board of Directors, Congressional Medal of Honor Foundation.
- Veterans of Foreign Wars *Citizenship Award* recipient 2006.
- Named "Man of the Year" by Boys Town of Italy and Mount Diablo Hospital Foundation.
- Honorary Citizen of the city of Shanghai, China (one of only two).
- Honorary Citizen of more than 20 other Chinese cities in recognition for supporting, establishing and contributing to natural history and science museums throughout China.
- Honorary President of Qingdao Binhai University.
- Founder of Wheelchair Foundation, which has given away nearly one million wheelchairs, free of charge, in more than 150 countries worldwide.
- Founder, Global Health and Education Foundation, providing clean drinking water, vision surgery, disaster relief, and humanitarian aid worldwide, including first response to the Haiti Earthquake disaster of 2010. Building science and technology and natural history museums throughout China.

Academic Honors
- Honorary Doctorate of Humanities, Brigham Young University, 2002.
- Honorary Doctorate, John F. Kennedy University, 2009.
- Honorary Professorship, Shenzhen University, Shenzhen, China.

Appendix B:
WHAT WE DO

The Global Health and Education Foundation is a 501(c)3 that was built on the success of the Wheelchair Foundation, a non-profit organization founded by Kenneth E. Behring in 2000 and now a division of GHEF. GHEF was established to identify, create and oversee multiple operations that specialize in providing aid to international health- and education-related areas of need with a goal of creating new leaders. It is a united network of charitable organizations dedicated to eliminating water-related disease, providing hope, mobility and freedom and expanding basic education and economic development opportunities around the world. You can find more information about all of our programs at *www.ghefoundation.org*.

Health

The Wheelchair Foundation, launched in 2000, is a nonprofit organization leading an international effort to create awareness of the needs and abilities of people with physical disabilities, to promote the joy of giving, create global friendship, and to deliver a wheelchair to every child, teen and adult in the world who needs one but cannot afford one. Thanks to the generous support of individual donors, corporations and humanitarian organizations, the Wheelchair Foundation delivers hope, mobility and independence to physically disabled people, allowing them to lead more productive lives and contribute to their communities, as well as providing help and relief for their families and caregivers. For more information, visit *www.wheelchairfoundation.org.*

Operation Global Vision, launched in 2008, is a partnership between GHEF and Lions Clubs International. Its mission is to alleviate the suffering caused by cataract blindness in the poorest areas of the world. The partnership strives to raise awareness and funding to stop this reversible form of blindness. Its goal is to perform 275,000 cataract surgeries over three years.

The Safe Drinking Water Project, launched in 2006, is a nonprofit program that addresses safe drinking water issues in the rural areas of China, with the joint efforts of China Disabled Persons' Federation (CDPF) and Chinese Academy of Science (CAS). The project seeks to eliminate water-related diseases and disability for future generations by setting up water purification systems in needy areas and providing clean water to local communities. In this work, GHEF brings its sustainability project management expertise and provides funding for purification water systems and spare parts for the first three years. CAS provides the technical support, including identifying places with need, analyzing water quality, defining water treatment processes and conducting project scientific research. CDPF is responsible for the project execution as it has mature local project practice.

Education and Museums

The Blackhawk Museum, Kenneth Behring's first museum venture, helped teach him about the power of museums to educate. The museum is home to one of the world's major collections of classic automobiles. You can learn more about it at *www.blackhawkmu-*

seum.org. He also supported a car museum in China, the *Shanghai Automobile Museum*. For more information on it, visit *http://www. shautocity.com/english/jcbl.htm*.

The Smithsonian Institution in Washington, DC, is the recipient of a $100 million pledge from Kenneth Behring for exhibitions about U.S. history and nature. In 2003, the Kenneth E. Behring Family Hall of Mammals opened in the Smithsonian National Museum of Natural History. Kenneth Behring subsequently supported two exhibitions at the National Museum of American History: "The American Presidency: A Glorious Burden" and "The Price of Freedom: Americans at War." In recognition of this gift, the building that houses the National Museum of American History was designated as the "Kenneth E. Behring Center." Learn more about his Smithsonian support at *http://naturalhistory.si.edu* and *http://americanhistory.si.edu*.

Through GHEF, Kenneth Behring is now supporting animal exhibitions in *museums in China*. His personal support began in 2004 with the donation of a spider collection to the Shanghai Science and Technology Museum for a new Spider Hall. He later donated animal specimens to natural history museums in Dalian and Beijing. He continues to work with museums throughout China to improve natural history education through the museum experience. You can learn more about this work at *http://www.ghefoundation.org/museums*.

Kenneth Behring provided funding for the *Principal Leadership Institute* at the University of California, Berkeley, in 2000 to provide scholarships to teachers in its Graduate School of Education as part of the Kenneth E. Behring Institute for Educational Improvement. The Principal Leadership Institutes, one at UC Berkeley and one at UCLA, were established by the University of California in response to the state's mandate to provide world-class management training to California's public school principals and to further the cause of education reform, especially in urban schools. For more information on the PLI, visit *http://gse.berkeley.edu/policy-organization-measurement-evaluation/pli*.

In 2009, Kenneth Behring and his wife, Pat, agreed to provide financial support to **National History Day**, which engages junior and senior high school students in history through research projects and local, state and national competitions. Each year, about 600,000 students and 25,000 teachers participate in NHD events, which help bring history alive for participants. For more information on NHD, visit *www.NHD.org*.

As a result of the success of NHD and his interest in nature and the natural sciences, Kenneth Behring and the GHEF launched **Global Natural History Day** in 2012. Modeled on NHD, it encourages better learning of the natural world and the lessons it offers mankind through research projects that also help develop critical, analytical and other skills. For more information, visit *www.gnhd.org*.

Leadership Development

In addition to the Principal Leadership Institute, which helps turn teachers into leaders, Kenneth Behring is formulating plans for programs to find and develop young people for high-level leadership positions in the future. Organizations may include a Behring Leadership Academy and a Behring Leadership Institute. For news and developments, visit *www.ghefoundation.org*.

Contact Information

Global Health and Education Foundation
3820 Blackhawk Road
Danville, California 94506   USA
Toll Free: (877) 378-3839
Local: (925) 736-8234
FAX: (925) 648-0163
Email: info@ghefoundation.org

The Wheelchair Foundation
3820 Blackhawk Road
Danville, California 94506 USA
Toll-Free: (877) 378-3839
North America:(925) 736-8234
FAX:(925) 648-0163
E-mail: info@wheelchairfoundation.org

Wheelchair Foundation China
Room 501, Building 10
600 North Shaanxi Rd.
Jing An District, Shanghai, 200041
Telephone: 86-21 6093 7866
Fax: 86-21 6093 7860
www.wheelchairfoundation.org.cn/

Appendix C:
FRIENDS AND SUPPORTERS

The Global Health and Education Foundation works with many individuals, companies and organizations to deliver education, good health and mobility to people around the world. The Foundation is grateful for all of the financial and other support they provide for its mission and looks forward to working with them for years to come. Here are a few of them:

Rotary Clubs and Rotarians
www.rotary.org

Since 2001, Rotary Clubs, Districts and individual Rotarians have sponsored the delivery of hundreds of thousands of wheelchairs to dozens of countries around the world. To date, Rotarians from every one of the 50 United States and every province of Canada have participated in the Wheelchair Foundation mission. Ken Behring is a member of the Rotary Club of Foster City, California.

The Church of Jesus Christ of Latter-Day Saints
www.lds.org

The very first "Global Partner" in the Wheelchair Foundation's mission to bring hope, mobility and freedom into the lives of people with physical disabilities was The Church of Jesus Christ of Latter-day Saints. The members of the LDS Church are building on a long and established tradition of compassion and charity by reaching out to help those who are in need of a better life.

China Disabled Persons' Federation

www.cdpf.org.cn/english/about.htm

The CDPF represents more than 60 million people with various categories of disabilities in China, including the physically disabled. The organization's goals are to promote humanitarianism and to protect the human rights of persons with disabilities. It also ensures their equal participation in society, their contribution to economic growth and their social development, as well as their equal share in the material and cultural achievements of China. CDPF has established chapters in most communities throughout the country.

The China Charity Federation
www.chinacharity.cn.net

China Ministry of Civil Affairs
www.mca.gov.cn

Chinese Academy of Sciences
http://english.cas.cn

California Academy of Sciences
http://www.calacademy.org/

Lions Clubs
www.lionsclubs.org

Oakland Athletics
www.oaklandathletics.com

Knights of Columbus
www.kofc.org

ChevronTexaco
www.chevrontexaco.com

"Global Partners"
$5,000,000+
Kenneth E. Behring Foundation
Rotary Clubs & Rotarians
The Church of Jesus Christ of Latter-Day Saints
U.S. Department of Defense
U.S. Department of State

"Founders Circle"
$1,000,000
China Charity Federation
China Disabled Persons' Federation
Fundación Telmex
Smithsonian Magazine
The Hofmann Foundation
WF Golf Tournament
Wheelchair Foundation Canada
Wheelchair Foundation UK
Wine for Wheels

"Benefactor"
$500,000
Ability Through Mobility
Chevron Corporation
Gordon Holmes / Lloyd & Louise / Streetwise

Henry E. Niles Foundation
KEB Collections
Knights of Columbus
Lee Roy Denson Trust
Ralph & Betty Englestad
Scharleen H. Colant Estate
The Oakland Athletics Community Fund

"Circle of Freedom"
$250,000
Cal Poly Clubs
Crystal Cathedral Ministries
David Walters
Don Williams & Ritchie Clyne
El Desarollo Integra
Hyundai
Ron & Marianne Dreisbach / Dreisbach Enterprises
Ronald Merritt / Bond Manufacturing
Sister Cities International

"Givers of Hope"
$100,000
Altria Group, Inc.
American Jewish Joint Distribution Committee
Monegasque Association "Les Enfants de Frankie"
Catherine B. Reynolds Foundation
C.I.L.S.A.
David E. Behring Family
Ed & Kirsten Boyce
Eric Rudney
Fondo Unido Rotario de Mexico
Fundación Pro Integración

Fundación Vamos México
George Gouveia Trust
Hee Dahl Park / Tiny Share of Field Activity
John & Linda Ribiero Jr.
Johnson & Johnson
Keiretsu Forum
Kevin & Janice Gillespie
Martha Sam Hertelendy, Paul Hertelendy & Family
Meehan Family Foundation
Million Dollar Round Table
Samaritan's Purse
Samsung
Seton Institute
Sid & Gigi Hendricks
Sir Durward Knowles
State of New York
Steven Polkow & Mara Hook
The Chatlos Foundation
The Semnani Foundation
Thomas A. Seeno Foundation
Tim & Kathy Eller
Val & Belia Nunes
VN Help
Wayne Clark
Wheelchair Foundation Australia

Other supporters have included:

Abbas I. Yousef Foundation
Behring Sons Foundation
Christopher Reeve Paralysis Foundation
The Greek Orthodox Church

The Knights of Malta
Major League Baseball
MetLife
Ronald McDonald House Charities
The Royal Family Foundation of Saudi Arabia
Seaton Institute
Sisters of Charity
Wells Fargo Foundation

Appendix D:
OUR TEAM

I launched the Wheelchair Foundation in June 2000 as a 501(c)3 nonpartisan, nondenominational, nonprofit organization. I later created the Global Health and Education Foundation and folded the Wheelchair Foundation into it. Here is a partial list of the people who have made our mission a success:

California Headquarters

Annette Anderson is an executive assistant to Ken Behring and is Regional Operations Director for the Middle East. After working for the Behrings as a household manager and assistant, she joined the Foundation when it launched in 2000. Her experience as a distribution, warehouse and quality control manager for an industrial company helped prepare her for her work at the Foundation, where those functions are important to operations and deliveries. She has been on dozens of wheelchair distributions, calling them a "wonderful thing, an instant life-changing experience" for both the recipient and the team member. She has been joined on distributions by her daughter, Tara, who works part-time on Foundation donor relations.

David Behring has served as the President of the Wheelchair Foundation since 2003. Before that, he was the president of the Blackhawk Automotive Museum, a Smithsonian Institution affiliate that is one of the most spectacular classic automobile collections in the world. David spent five years (1993–1997) as president of the Seattle Seahawks and was a member of the NFL Finance Committee. A graduate of Princeton University and the University of Miami Law School, he spent most of his business career in homebuilding and development in California. David, a Rotarian, has been active in both professional and community service organizations for almost 30 years and has served on numerous boards during this period. He is a member of the Smithsonian's National Museum of American History board as well as the board of National History Day.

Jeff Behring, Director of Special Events, helps to "sow the seeds" of the Foundation and its work around the world. He is also a property manager and a general contractor, building custom homes as well as semi-custom homes and commercial and warehouse buildings. He also does tenant improvement work. Jeff is a Rotarian and a Paul Harris Fellow with the Danville, California, Rotary Club. He received a Bachelor of Arts degree from Southern Methodist University in 1980, concentrating in real estate and finance. He is married and has four children.

Steve Beinke is the president and a member of the board of the Global Health and Education Foundation and a board member of the Wheelchair Foundation. He is one of my key advisors in philanthropy and a long-time business partner who I have worked with for more than 40 years. Steve is the current president of Behring Group Ltd. and the Blackhawk Group of Companies. His work with Blackhawk helped establish our firm as a premier development company that has produced numerous large-scale, master-planned golf course communities, multifamily housing, senior active adult communities, commercial office developments, regional and neighborhood retail centers, and mixed-use developments in California and Washington. His other nonprofit work has included being a trustee of the Mount

Diablo Hospital Foundation and president of the Kiwanis Club of San Ramon.

Charli Butterfield came to us from the airline industry, which culminated with a career as a commercial aviator. Charli joined our organization as a pilot for the Seattle Seahawks in 1992. Charli is responsible for flight operations and international event coordination with NGOs around the globe. She has participated in all of my humanitarian efforts aboard my aircraft, including shipping educational materials and clothing to Africa, shipping wheelchairs around the world and coordinating important meetings with heads of state. In addition, she is currently responsible for directing the procurement of taxidermied animals for the museums in Asia we are working with in the Global Health and Education Foundation. In 2012, Charli was honored as "Volunteer of the Year" by the Wheelchair Foundation at its annual charity gala.

Eva Carleton, Director of Operations for Latin America and the Caribbean for the Wheelchair Foundation, joined us in 2003. Eva manages all wheelchair deliveries to Latin America and the Caribbean, the Foundation's second-busiest region. Her primary focus is the efficient delivery and distribution of wheelchairs through capacity building, facilitating between donors and in-country partner organizations, project funding, relationship building and problem solving. Eva holds a Master's of Law and Diplomacy degree from the Fletcher School at Tufts University, where she specialized in negotiation and conflict resolution and humanitarian aid. Eva speaks English, Spanish, German and French. Before joining the Wheelchair Foundation, Eva worked on CARE's human rights framework for development and mediated disputes for the Massachusetts Department of Telecommunications and Energy.

Tiffany Camacho is the Wheelchair Foundation's public education manager. She joined the organization in 2002 to help educate people about the worldwide need for wheelchairs and the Foundation's mission. Tiffany handles donor inquires and shipping of all educational materials to potential donors and all Foundation offices. Tiffany's attention to detail is applied when creating personalized donor marketing kits and executing the elements needed for conferences, events and direct mailings. She now has also joined the Global Health and Education Team to assist with upcoming projects.

Dyan Yun Han, CFP®, has been the chief investment officer for Kenneth E. Behring Investments and financial director for Global Health and Education Foundation. Dyan has been holding the Certified Finanical Planner™ professional designation and is currently a CFA Level II candidate. With over 12 years of experience in the financial industry as a wealth management professional, Dyan has been working with me on the overall equity portfolio management, including the portfolio building, ongoing securities analysis and risk management. Dyan used to work with a registered investment management firm with $800 million AUM (assets under management) as a financial advisor. Before that, she worked for TD Waterhouse (name changed to TD Ameritrade after a merger) in San Francisco as an investment consultant. Over $500 million in high net worth relationships was handled during her tenure there. She used to hold FINRA licenses: Series 6, 7, 9, 10, 63 and 66. She earned her Personal Financial Planning Certificate from UC Berkeley Extension and holds her BA degree from a university from China. She is bilingual in Chinese (Mandarin) and passionate about traveling around the world.

Joel Hodge has been with the Wheelchair Foundation since 2000 as the program director. He also works on Global Health and

Education Foundation projects worldwide. Joel has traveled the world extensively distributing wheelchairs and as a representative of the Foundation. Joel received a Bachelor's of Science in Biology from Missouri State University and has worked in the biotech sector and in private banking, as well as for the Federal Reserve Bank of Kansas City. He and his wife, Molly, reside in Marin, California, with their two sons.

Gerry Riley is the transportation and logistics manager for the Wheelchair Foundation. After a career in computer hardware and software support, he joined the Foundation in 2003 to help get wheelchairs manufactured and delivered. He said he initially experienced a pretty steep learning curve getting familiar with the intricacies of international ocean freight. His earlier skill set and engineering degree came in handy, though, as he was able to pull together disparate functions and data and automate much of the shipping process. He was also instrumental in assisting with the design of our transportation database. He enjoys working at an organization whose mission and very reason for existence is to give help to those in need.

Marsha Warner, CPA, is our controller. She started working with the Wheelchair Foundation in 2001. She works closely with auditors to set up policies and procedures in accounting. She worked for nine years in public accounting for a local firm in Fremont, California, and 12 years in the construction and insurance industries as a controller. She is married with two children.

China Office

Angie Shen is the chief representative of the Global Health and Education Foundation and the Wheelchair Foundation in China, where she has spearheaded a number of community outreach and advocacy initiatives such as the Red Wheelchair project and Mobile Museum. She and her team also successfully launched the Global Natural History Day in three major cities in China after only four months of planning. After joining my organization in 2004, Angie moved back to Shanghai in 2006 to take over our operations, including my business entity, the Behring Group China, where she also serves as CEO and as a member of the Board of Directors. She has been instrumental in brokering deals for land acquisition and entitlement, maintaining positive government and public relations and serving in a sales and marketing management role for The Sanctuary at Dongtan project in Shanghai. Before joining the Behring Group, Angie worked in the banking industry in the San Francisco Bay area. Angie graduated from Saint Mary's College of California in 2002 with a degree in Finance and Economics.

Florida Office

Jack Drury met me in 1960 when he moved to Ft. Lauderdale, Florida. I was a builder, and the Drury family needed a home. The purchase of the home led me to hire Jack's advertising firm to handle marketing for Behring Properties. When I moved to California, Jack stayed in Florida. In 2000, Jack, who was retired, called to congratulate me on creating the Wheelchair Foundation. I wanted to take advantage of Jack's talents, and a month later, he opened the Southeast Office of the Wheelchair Foundation in Fort Lauderdale. He oversees Wheelchair Foundation activities in the southeastern United States, South and Central America and the Caribbean.

Nevada Office

Don Williams oversees wheelchair distributions in Nevada as a friend and volunteer of the Foundation. The Nevada chapter has distributed more than 2,000 wheelchairs in the state. Through his friendship with the late Nevada businessman Ralph Englestad, who was a native of North Dakota, the chapter also has distributed 2,100 wheelchairs in that state. Don's full-time work is buying and selling classic cars; he is the world's leading expert on prewar classics. But he said he fell in love with what I was doing around the world and has tried to help us in any way he can, including raising more than $1 million for the Wheelchair Foundation.

International Board of Advisors

Our Board of Advisors includes two of my closet friends, **King Juan Carlos of Spain** and his wife, **Queen Sofia**. Both are active in philanthropy. Through the various foundations of which he is patron, the King personally supports the creation and development of new technology in Spain, promotes initiatives in the areas of economics, business, research and social advances and encourages solidarity at all levels of society in Spain. The Queen devotes much of her time to social and welfare activities. She is the Executive President of the Queen Sofia Foundation. She is also the Honorary President of the Foundation for Aid for Drug Users and of the Royal Trust for the Handicapped, as well as of various cultural and musical institutions, including the Queen Sofia Higher School of Music. She also participates in a number of international projects for the promotion of rural women and for the development of micro-credits for the disadvantaged.